For Nathan, with ~~~~
wonderful leadership during our week
in Guatemala. It was great fun
being a Gator-aide and sharing coffee
one special evening together! Blessings
on your marriage and your ministry —
                Carol

YOU MATTER TO ME

CAROL J. SHERMAN, PhD

YOU MATTER TO ME
The Unvarnished Truth about Love

TATE PUBLISHING
AND ENTERPRISES, LLC

You Matter to Me
Copyright © 2016 by Carol J. Sherman, PhD. All rights reserved.

No part of this publication may be reproduced, stored in a retrieval system or transmitted in any way by any means, electronic, mechanical, photocopy, recording or otherwise without the prior permission of the author except as provided by USA copyright law.

This book is designed to provide accurate and authoritative information with regard to the subject matter covered. This information is given with the understanding that neither the author nor Tate Publishing, LLC is engaged in rendering legal, professional advice. Since the details of your situation are fact dependent, you should additionally seek the services of a competent professional.

FROM THE SCIENCE OF TRUST: EMOTIONAL ATTUNEMENT FOR COUPLES by John M. Gottman. Copyright © 2011 by John M. Gottman. Used by permission of W. W. Norton & Company, Inc.

The opinions expressed by the author are not necessarily those of Tate Publishing, LLC.

Published by Tate Publishing & Enterprises, LLC
127 E. Trade Center Terrace | Mustang, Oklahoma 73064 USA
1.888.361.9473 | www.tatepublishing.com

Tate Publishing is committed to excellence in the publishing industry. The company reflects the philosophy established by the founders, based on Psalm 68:11,
"*The Lord gave the word and great was the company of those who published it.*"

Book design copyright © 2016 by Tate Publishing, LLC. All rights reserved.
Cover design by Joana Quilantang
Interior design by Gram Telen
Illustrations by Scott Sherman

Published in the United States of America
ISBN: 978-1-68028-562-8
Family & Relationships / General
15.11.25

Dedicated to my parents, Thomas and Carolyn Jones, who were the first instruments of God's grace in my life, and who first taught me how to love.

Acknowledgements

I want to express my gratitude to my husband, Bob, who has been my life companion in learning mutual love. Thank you for thirty wonderful years and for all the ones ahead of us.

My sons, Scott and Joe, who have added so much joy to my life. Thank you for all you've taught me about love and for the many mistakes you've forgiven along the way. Special thanks to Scott for his patience and talent in illustrating this book with and for me.

Renee Garrett, dear friend and colleague, who prodded me in 2007 to create and teach a college-level class about love where I could try out my framework on "the public," refine it and solicit examples of love in action. Your continual encouragement, input, and feedback have been Challenge Love in action.

Don S. Browning, deceased, my mentor and teacher who helped redirect my path.

The countless dear friends who have given me so much Nurture Love and Challenge Love on my journey.

The many students who have graciously allowed me to use their examples of Nurture Love and Challenge Love to illustrate my framework.

My countless clients who have allowed me to enter the sacred space of their hearts where I have seen more fully love's power to wound and heal, nurture, and help us meet life's challenges.

Contents

Preface 11

Introduction: Some New Glasses 13

Part 1: Some Preliminaries

1 What Do I Mean by Love? 29
2 Love Builds Up, Anxiety Disrupts 35
3 The Ambivalence at the Heart of Love 41

Part 2: The Goal of Love—Love Builds Up

4 The Components of a Resilient Self 57

Part 3: Love Pays Attention

5 Attunement—the Way to Build and Maintain Trust 97

Part 4: Love in Action—Love Treasures

Treasuring 111
The Nurture Loves 117
6 Love Nurtures by Actively Cherishing a Loved One 125
7 Love Nurtures by Sustaining the Loved One 145

The Challenge Loves 155
8 Challenge Love Supports the Loved One 159

9   Challenge Love Coaches/Teaches the Loved One 175
10 Challenge Love Pollinates with Insights, Perspective and Inspiration 189
11 Challenge Love Confronts Differences Respectfully and Carefully 197
12 Challenge Love Takes a Firm Stand Against a Loved One's Destructive Actions 217

Concluding Comments 227

Appendices
  Appendix A: A Really Short Version of Erikson's Stage Theory 231
  Appendix B: Puzzle It Out
    A way to communicate better 239
  Appendix C: Confronting Issues Respectfully 261
  Appendix D: Self-soothing Techniques 267

Glossary of Terms 271

Notes 283

Works Cited and Further Resources 293

Preface

When I was in college psychology classes studying child development, the women's movement was in full swing. Many women wanted to be freed from the cultural assumption that it was their job to raise the children. Much was being written about whether men could or would do a good job nurturing very young children. Much was also being written about what was driving women to want to pursue careers outside the realm of homemaking and child-rearing. The 1970s and '80s were a time of culture wars between women who wanted no children at all, those who wanted to combine motherhood with other careers, and women who held motherhood and homemaking as their sacred calling.

That was the climate in which I began to think intentionally about love, asking myself "what kind of love do children really need?" By the time I finished graduate school and started practicing as a psychotherapist, I had married and was the mother of two small boys. What I had learned about love by growing up surrounded by it, and then studying what the experts said was now guiding me in my home and in my work with clients. I was crystallizing a framework for understanding what I had been learning. I no longer focused exclusively on what children need from their parents. I could see more and more clearly that the same types of issues and challenges come around repeatedly throughout life and while the style of delivery must change as we get older, the need for love to be concretely expressed in a variety of ways does not disappear. It doesn't even fade, really, even though many people teach themselves to pretend otherwise.

Throughout life, human beings need two very different kinds of love. We need to be accepted and cared for just as we are, often called "unconditional love." And we also need to be encouraged, helped, and even prodded to grow and change. Initially, I saw these as maternal and paternal approaches to parenting, but a wise mentor gently but firmly showed me that women and men are capable of both ways of loving even though one way may come more readily than the other, leading them to lean toward one more than the other. She helped me see that naming these two categories for their primary characteristics would be far more helpful in the larger picture, allowing men and women to acknowledge their default mode and become more conscious of times their loved one would be better served if they "leaned the other direction." "Nurture Love" and "Challenge Love" have therefore become the names I use for these two encompassing categories of love, each manifested by certain types of actions that directly affect the loved one.

When I began teaching a college class on love in 2008, I introduced students to my framework for what love looks like in action. In particular, I had them recall specific instances of receiving the various kinds of love and identify how those had fostered in them any of the core ego strengths identified more than half a century ago by psychologist Erik Erikson. Time and again, their papers have shown how Nurture Love and Challenge Love in action foster the ego strengths that create a more resilient self—a core of personal identity that feels authentic and integrated—in the loved one.

If you or someone you know missed out on the basics about love for whatever reason, I think you'll find this book helpful.

Introduction: Some New Glasses

"I don't really know what love is, or what it looks like." For many years now, clients have told me and shown me this sad truth at the center of their lives. They talk about a feeling, attraction, and attachments they wish they could get into or out of. Many of them go through one relationship after another with people who don't know any more about real love than they do. Love worthy of the name wasn't modeled in their homes growing up, and usually what they now call by the name of *love* is a counterfeit, one of many forms of unhealthy attachment that was the best their parents, caregivers, or relationship partners could do.

I've looked for resources to give these clients some clues, but most of the books I've found are too long or too complicated. People who don't have many clues need to start with the basics. They need a primer about love. So here's what I'm offering: a simple, fairly fast read filled with lively examples and illustrations to make it all accessible for the uninitiated. That way, if you find it helpful and want to ask someone you know to read it, there's half a chance they'll give it a try.

If you were fortunate enough to grow up in a home with people who loved you well, you probably picked up a lot of the art of loving without even realizing it. So maybe you do have a clue about love and you picked this book up because you know you're not on solid ground yet. Or maybe the person with whom you're in a relationship doesn't "get it" at all and you wish you could explain to them what's missing for you.

It's no secret that learning how to love well comes most easily by being loved well. But where does that leave the rest of the population, the ones who weren't loved well? One young man told me the only clues he had were from reruns of *The Cosby Show* on TV, and it was obvious that trying to put those faint images and snippets into practice in his marriage wasn't going very well. He knew the Huxtables' treatment of each other had felt right and good, but he couldn't articulate the values embedded in it and hadn't been able to make them his own. He didn't know how to.

If you missed out on "good enough" parenting[1] and haven't been able to apprentice to someone who loves others well, you probably need a teacher to give you guidance about how to do it. That's where I come in. Even if you did internalize a decent working model for how to treat one another in life-giving ways, it can be hard to put into words what you know intuitively, and it's especially hard to describe what's missing to someone who didn't grow up receiving it. Sometimes we feel embarrassed asking for things that are so very basic. It makes us feel childish. But these outward evidences of love are the warp and woof of a tapestry we weave together in relationships that have staying power and if they are missing, we need a way to find them and add them into the pictures we are creating.

In this book, I'm going to provide you with three pairs of glasses, three sets of corrective lenses to help you learn to love the people who matter to you. Each pair of glasses brings into focus some important clues about love. As you'll see, conveying "You matter to me—*you*, for your own sake, not just because you meet my needs"—is the essence of loving well.

After some preliminaries in part one, we'll look at glasses created by Erik Erikson. In part two, I'll use this developmental psychologist's lenses to show you that a relationship worthy of the name of *love* has certain predictable outcomes. Love brings about the well-being of the loved one. Erikson describes how certain core "ego strengths" develop in a child when there is good enough parenting, strengths he uses word pairs to describe: basic trust and hope, autonomy and willpower, initiative and a sense of purpose; industry (diligence) and competencies; all of which become ingredients in crystallizing a sense of identity and selfhood to which you can be loyal. In this book I will be using the term *self* as if it were an entity or agent and I will speak of *components* that make up that entity. In truth it's probably more accurate to think of self as an ongoing activity of being in the moment and integrating what's taking place. But in order to *do* that well, a person needs to have the faith, willpower, purpose, sense of competencies, and crystallizing sense of personhood Erikson helps us understand.[2]

That sense of identity continues to develop and strengthen when trust makes it possible to know and be known in intimate relationships with peers, a capacity Erikson calls *mutuality*. Forming a committed, loving relationship in marriage is the garden in which such intimacy flourishes most fully, although deep platonic friendships with either male or female friends are also abundantly rich environments for mutuality to grow. The more available all of these resources are to an adult self, the more likely that person is to care well for the next generation and the world around them (generativity). When people look back on their lives, those who have had the benefit of these components of a resilient self tend to feel their lives had integrity, by and large, and they seem to have gained wisdom that puts things in perspective.

Some critics have argued Erikson's developmental theory isn't *universal*, that these particular traits are valued primarily in the Western world. While that may be true[3], they are most certainly the building blocks of a sense of self-worth among the clients, family, and friends I encounter in my practice and life. When a child begins to develop them early in relationship with parents and other caregivers, they[4] have a more than decent chance of becoming a relatively well-functioning adult, capable of appropriately taking other people's needs and wants into account. Not only do they become capable of intimacy and care later in life (the terms Erikson uses for adult ego strengths which are actually forms of loving)[5], but they are more free to love another person well because they are not preoccupied with anxieties created by shaky or missing building blocks within the self.

I'll show you how the cultivation and support of these ego strengths is at the heart of in the following:

- parenting young children
- parenting teenagers
- helping romantic love mature into life-giving married love
- devoted friendships
- loving our aging parents as their ability to sustain themselves diminishes.

It's my premise that if you really love someone—whether it's a child, teenager, or an adult—you want to help them develop and use these ego strengths so they can experience self-worth and go on to make a positive difference in the world around them.

The second pair of glasses comes from a current researcher and relationship therapist named John Gottman. In part three, we'll use his lenses to look far more closely at how attunement is at the core of *trust* in important relationships throughout life, not only in childhood. It's well-established that less than 10 percent of communication resides in the actual words a person speaks. In order to fully understand another person, we rely on interpreting their facial expressions, tone of voice, and body language. This is why emoticons were rapidly created when e-mails (and then texts) came along—to provide some of the visual or auditory information the recipient would notice if the message were delivered in person. People on the autism spectrum have trouble picking up and accurately interpreting these nonverbal social messages.

Attunement is learned from experiences of having someone tune in to you. It is a process that helps you discover what you're experiencing within yourself and then, by practicing feedback loops with other people, you discover whether you are reading their nonverbals accurately or not.

As you will see in chapter 5, attunement is a skill that can be taught and learned, but as with other languages, it is most easily learned in childhood. I include it in this book because our culture's increasing reliance on electronic snippets of communication is rapidly stripping away the sustained interpersonal in-person experiences within which attunement is learned. When parents of young children are paying attention to smartphones, laptops, iPads, etc., they are not attuning to their children, so those children are not part of a mutual feedback loop of learning about each other's inner world. Even when two people are together in the same place these days, their attention is often, if not usually, divided rather than focused on receiving the fullness of what that other person is communicating. As my twenty-six-year-old son pointed out in a recent conversation, "loving another person is complicated" and it remains to be seen whether a generation adept at carrying on multiple electronic conversations at once will be attuned enough to carry on the kind of face-to-face, in-depth conversations required for intimacy to grow. Although attunement *can* be used for harmful purposes by a person with a selfish hidden agenda, in the service of someone whose goal is loving another person well, it is an essential skill for picking up all the little clues that can guide us.

Unlike so many relationship gurus who create counseling models from their idealistic beliefs about what *should* work to make relationships strong, Gottman's approach has come from more than thirty years of observing couples closely, noticing their interactions, and discovering over time how those ways of taking each other into account—or not taking each other into account—are correlated with stability or breakups. He uses a different language than mine, but he's essentially established that subtle and blatant messages of "you matter to me" or "you don't matter to me" identifiable early in a relationship are excellent predictors of a long and basically satisfying marriage... or of a divorce.

Gottman's insights apply to adults who are trying to create intimacy and mutuality and demonstrate care, whether they realize those are their goals or not. In parts one and two, I will have explained in depth how the seed of a child's selfhood grows and strengthens within the garden of trustworthy, supportive relationships. You will arrive at part three understanding that when people arrive at chronological adulthood with weak or missing ego strengths, they are likely to be preoccupied with hiding "their flat sides," or compensating for them in whatever usually problematic ways they managed to come up with. Under these conditions, it is practically impossible to be attuned to a partner's well-being to the degree necessary to have a truly mature adult love relationship.

Mutuality as Erikson defines it is the ability to love in such a way that the partner's well-being matters just as much as one's own. It is quite an accomplishment, really, and it seems increasingly scarce these days. Contemporary culture's revolving-door approach to relationships makes it challenging to figure out what *commitment* actually means in today's relational world. Judging from how quickly hook-ups and move-ins take place in the world my clients and students describe, trust doesn't appear to be particularly important in these decisions.

Then, too, many of my clients bring a mishmash of hopes and expectations to even the idea of committed relationship. Often, their standards were shaped by parents who never married or who divorced, and then by watching throughout their childhood and teen years as those parents related to a series of new live-in partners. Occasionally, I hear positive stories about one of these adults who passed through a client's or student's life, but far more often, the impact was a further undermining of ego strengths, particularly of basic trust.

Increasingly, I see evidence that people bring to their relationships the same mentality they bring to the following:

- fast food (it satisfies the appetite quickly, so what if there's no nutritional value?);
- disposable razors (use it once or twice and throw it away);
- planned obsolescence (nothing lasts; just plan on replacing it in six months or a few years at most); and
- constantly and rapidly updatable technology (as soon as a new and better one is available, I'll dump this one and get it).

Even in this culture, I see in my clients of all ages an awareness that the presence of trust remains at the very heart of any relationship that has value. They sense this to be true even if they don't have such a relationship anywhere in their lives. They may be cynical about other people and even about their own capacity to be trustworthy, but they recognize that *if they could have it* at the heart of a relationship, it would be worth more than gold.

Gottman's findings about trust are thoroughly relevant to every person trying to sort out whether to stay in a particular relationship or not. Couples deciding whether to extend a hook-up into something more may look primarily at whether the sex was satisfying, whether they had fun hanging out together, whether the other person's friends were tolerable to be around. But if and when a person does start thinking about long-term commitment—even pseudocommitment—they start asking themselves, "Is this relationship good for me? Do they really take my well-being into account, or are they mostly selfish?" As you may have realized, at this point the person has crossed over into actively wondering about trust. To use my language, they're asking "Do I trust that I really matter to him/her?"

Gottman's research shows some very simple, but powerful findings about what builds and erodes trust in a relationship.[5] He has worked closely with his wife, Julie, to create an approach to couples therapy based on his research findings about what makes a relationship solid. My primary focus in this book will be on his discovery and insight that *attunement*—which comes naturally to some, but is a skill that can be taught and learned—is the heart of establishing and maintaining interpersonal trust. Day in and day out, adults and children alike are making what Gottman calls "bids" for connection with the important people around them— subtle or open requests for a connection of some kind. How those important people respond to those bids communicates spoken and unspoken volumes about love and about what I call *mattering*. And it turns out that many of the findings about how children form secure or ambivalent attachments to their parents are relevant to adult relationships as well.[6]

Gottman's observational research also identified four toxic attitudes/behaviors that both signal and contribute to the disappearance of love: contempt, criticism, defensiveness, and stonewalling. Because they are so clearly associated with "the end" of a loving relationship, he calls them "the Four Horsemen of the Apocalypse[8]." In essence, they are manifestations of an excessively self-centered point of view, evidence that the other person's well-being doesn't matter like it used to. Thankfully, people who want to swim against the current of their own selfish tendencies can and will resist these toxic behaviors.

Finally, in part four, I'll explain my own set of lenses for bringing love into focus. In a sense, they are trifocals or progressive lenses that allow us to see the interplay of the following:

- tenderhearted emotion denoted by the word *love*;
- an attitude of devotion to the loved one's well-being, which I maintain is love's essence; and
- actions by which the loved one knows devotion resides in the heart and mind of the "lover"—by which I mean "the one who loves". It's unfortunate that the term has been co-opted by the sex-and-romance dimension of love.[9]

Think about your interactions with any other person and ask yourself, "For what reason, to what extent, and in what way does this other person matter to me?" Many philosophies and religions advocate treating other people well based on everything from reason, practicality, and enlightened self-interest; to the assertion that we are all family (children of the same Father God); to the belief that we are commanded by God/Jesus to "love our neighbors," making it a matter of obedience or duty. When I think of the attitude that motivates us to take another person into account, I picture a motivation gradient running from head to heart.

I call that heart-based end *treasuring* and I use the verb *treasure* to capture the experience of having a place for another person in your heart.

Somehow, inexplicably, your sense of self has opened up to include that person and though you may be embarrassed to admit it in these rather poetic terms, they are part of your treasure in life.

When this first happens, there are often physical sensations of a" tug on the heartstrings" or a swelling or aching in the chest, sensations we tend to equate with the emotion of love.[10] It literally feels like the organ in your chest is getting larger or opening its sliding door. The emotion and sensations can be delightful, painful, or both at the same time. Many people let these physical attachment sensations be their primary guide in relationships without crediting the importance of the other two strands of the braid. They enter relationships or exit them based entirely on these sensations. As we'll see later, you can experience the tenderheartedness without ever expressing it in such a way that the loved one knows you feel it. On the receiving side, you can know you are important to another person for any number of reasons, but there is an incomparable security in the knowledge that their heart has opened to let you in. I use the verb *cherish* for the actions that physically communicate this subjective treasuring reality to the loved one.

I use the verb *sustain* for those behaviors that meet the loved one's survival needs for food, clothing, shelter, protection, comfort, etc. Cherishing and sustaining are two kinds of behaviors that *nurture* the loved one's well-being just as they are. The person does nothing to earn them or deserve them. These gifts of grace come just because the person exists. They are forms of what I call *Nurture Love*.

There is a second overarching category of love I call *Challenge Love*. Challenge Love is motivated by the desire to help the loved one grow, learn, overcome obstacles, and develop their potential. You can think of Nurture Love as treasuring and sustaining the loved one's "being" (i.e., existence), while in contrast, the Challenge Loves help the loved one "become."

Challenge Love includes behaviors that *support* the loved one, providing encouragement and assistance of various types as they develop in self-initiated and self-chosen ways. Typically, these types of support are welcomed when they are offered in ways that fit the developmental needs of the loved one. If the one who loves has pertinent skills or knowledge, they may choose to give their time and energy to actively *coach or teach* the loved one. There's a third type of Challenge Love I call *pollinating* because the love giver brings insight about the loved one or inspiration that is a necessary catalyst for something new to happen. These three manifestations of love are usually fairly well-received since they more or less come alongside and move in the same direction the loved one is choosing to move. Or, in the case of pollinating, the loved one may be stalled out and the pollen helps them get moving again.

The other two types of Challenge Love behavior are invariably experienced as interference, making them the most difficult to carry out well. Our first experiences in life of being confronted by those who love us come in the form of discipline from our parents and other caregivers or teachers. Authority figures telling us to stop doing something, start doing something, or change the way we're doing something pervade our experience of life throughout childhood and adolescence. Because of this background, it can be very difficult later in life to effectively receive corrective/negative feedback from peers even if they respectfully ask for or suggest change. And when the delivery of that message is clumsy or overly critical, it often brings out the willfully resistant two-year-old or fourteen-year-old in us.

Obviously, some people criticize just because they enjoy finding fault or gaining advantage in a power struggle and that isn't love. But all of us do need the benefit of honest feedback and input from people who care about us as we go through life. Real love requires us to speak up when we experience a loved one as hurting themselves, getting off course, undermining their own goals, or as damaging their relationship with us through their behaviors. In those situations, we recognize an obstacle in the loved one's path and the manner in which we confront the loved one with our perspective can make all the difference in the world. Doing it effectively takes a lot of self-control and carefulness if it's going to be effective, and of all the things I try to teach clients, it's probably the most difficult. I'll share with you some of the tools I've found most helpful personally and professionally, including some skills recommended by the Gottmans.

If confronting and asking for change carefully and respectfully doesn't work, the only loving option that remains may be to *take a stand* against a loved one's damaging behaviors. Tough love has been described well in the recovery movement associated with addiction treatment. Within my framework, what's important to understand is that sometimes treasuring itself requires that the actions of Nurture Love be withheld in a last-ditch effort to save the loved one from self-destruction or to prevent a relationship from remaining abusive. These two forms of Challenge Love are essential parts of discipline in parent-child relationships, and they are also important elements of solid adult friendships, respectful work relationships, and strong marriages.

Cherishing, by its very definition, is the only action that requires the emotion known as love to be subjectively felt in the moment of action. The other Nurture Loves and Challenge Loves that contribute to the loved one's well-being can be and often are carried out regardless of whether we feel tenderness at that moment or not. In fact, the hallmark of treasuring someone is that we carry out the actions of love even when we don't feel like it at the moment.

As you may be realizing, I actually have a pretty broad and encompassing definition of love. While I'm primarily writing to help you more effectively love the people you personally treasure, if you take this approach with the people you work with, or even with whom you have casual acquaintance, you're likely to see some pretty fulfilling results.

Using examples from the lives of my students, I will help you see that ego strengths can and should be facilitated throughout life by the loving behaviors of people who care. It's never too late.

How Does It All Fit Together?

These seven core actions—cherishing, sustaining, supporting, coaching/teaching, pollinating, confronting in a respectful manner, and taking a stand—are the behaviors by which you can foster ego strengths in a loved one whether you treasure them personally or just recognize that all human beings are worthy of your help. Keeping the ego strengths in mind can help you fit your manner of sustaining, supporting, confronting, etc. to the particular situation. It can be difficult to discern which ego strength(s) are most in need of enhancement right now at this particular moment. For instance, there may be times when teaching a competency may be at odds with encouraging autonomy. Attunement is important in discerning what combination of Nurture Love or Challenge Love might fit the person's age and circumstances as you encourage the needed ego strength(s). Think about it: what's needed to foster autonomy in a forty-year-old who's been fired from their job looks very different from what's needed to foster it in a seventeen-year-old who prefers video games to hard work. It's also different from what's needed with a seventeen-year-old who is depressed because of low self-esteem. By coupling attunement skills with the big picture provided by Erikson, we can make better decisions in these situations.

I'm offering you three new sets of corrective lenses to help you do a better job of loving just about anyone who really matters to you. Here is your opportunity to change your whole approach to relationships, one that will ultimately change your life—for the better.

Part 1: Some Preliminaries

1

What Do I Mean by Love?

In its fullest and strongest form, love is a three-stranded braid of emotion, attitude, and actions. One strand without the others doesn't have nearly the strength and resilience as when all three are involved.

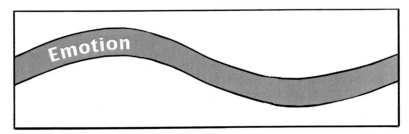

Emotion is what most people think of first when the word love is used, and that's one strand of the braid. Sometimes it's there from the start of a relationship, and sometimes it takes time to appear and grow. It's an embodied emotion by which I mean there's a physical experience that goes along it.[1] These sensations connected with the emotion of love are part of a mammal's limbic attachment system rather than its reproductive lust system. Whereas lust is an appetite (for sex), love is a desire for many other kinds of connection.

People describe the physical sensations of treasuring in a variety of ways like the following:

- an ache in your chest, sometimes described as "my heart melted" or a tug on your heart;
- an opening-up feeling in your chest as if the other person is becoming part of you, as if you're merging into one;
- your heart *skips a beat* when you see the loved one;
- a sensation of softening or tenderness in your chest;
- a glow of happiness and sense of well-being when you're with the person; and
- an almost magnetic pull to be in the presence of the loved one because you feel so good when you are around them.

Not all these sensations are experienced all the time, but most people will recognize these physical and emotional feelings as very prominent in the beginning of many love relationships of all kinds—parents and children, close friendships, and of course romantic attachments—and present, at least occasionally, throughout.

To varying degrees there is an attraction, an experience of being drawn toward the loved one. This is often accompanied by a subjective experience of "I need" that person. Love as emotion also includes a desire to give to that person[2]. These two inner realities actually feel very different physiologically and close examination reveals they are associated with different emotions even though we carelessly use love as a catchall for both. To say "I love you" and mean "I need you" carries an unspoken plea and a subtext of feeling vulnerable within the attachment. To say "I love you" and mean "out of what I have, I want to provide something that will add to your life" carries a subtext of feeling enriched and empowered by the attachment. This rarely discussed difference is behind many regrets when down the road, people realize they were hearing one thing when the other person was really saying another. Also, sometimes a person initially really likes the "you need me" part of being loved, only to discover later that the dependency is more of a burden than they expected.

As you will learn in chapter 6, attachment emotions while in love are uniquely intense, whether it is a parent in love with their baby, toddlers in love with their mommies, teenage crushes, or romantic pairings. It's normal for the intensity of these feelings to subside over time and for their nature to evolve, but the emotions don't disappear altogether unless the other two strands of the braid are neglected. What's more, when the other two strands are very present in the relationship, the more quiet emotions of appreciation and gratitude take up residence where infatuation (the addiction-like element) once dominated. When love's attitude and actions remain a priority, waves of treasuring continue to pass through often enough to keep a relationship vital.

Once a person experiences the heart-opening-up feelings of treasuring, their subjective sense of self is redefined and the circle expands to include that other person, i.e., they treasure them. Their well-being becomes of essential importance and so long as that person remains within the circle of tender treasuring, taking that person into account comes naturally and almost automatically. If that person is threatened somehow, your own *mama bear* or *papa bear* claws come out instantly to protect them.

Sometimes a client will tell me they still love their spouse but *are no longer in love with them* as a way of explaining why they fell in love with someone else or why they are divorcing. Usually, my initial hunch in those situations is that one or both marriage partners became careless or lazy about taking the other person into account when the infatuation subsided. In some cases, the arrival of the first baby redirected a mother's or even a father's focus to such an extent that the spouse felt pushed out of the circle of treasuring. The tenderness of appreciation and gratitude don't spring up automatically where infatuation used to be. They only take root and grow when the attitude of devotion as described below becomes a way of life and is recognized by the recipient as a blessing rather than an entitlement.

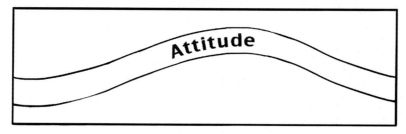

The second strand of the braid is the attitude toward the loved one, specifically an attitude of devotion to their well-being. One dictionary defines devotion as profound dedication and that is the sense in which I'm using it. Devotion is more than commitment. After all, you can make a commitment to another person to carry out a task on their behalf or pursue a shared goal together without caring about them as a person. It's also true that a person may be devoted to a loved one and not be consciously aware of the physical sensations of treasuring because experiences earlier in life taught them to ignore or deny those sensations and their meaning. You'll learn more about this in the chapter specifically devoted to cherishing.

In the realm of love, to be devoted to the loved one means their well-being matters to you in their own right apart from your own personal needs. Their fulfillment as a person is important to you even if it means sacrifices on your part. As an attitude, devotion is a willingness to extend yourself, to go out of your way to help your loved one thrive. [3]

What you may not have realized is that experiencing the emotion and sensations of love in your heart and having the attitude of devotion in your mind don't have any effect on the loved one at all. You may feel tenderhearted toward them and you may earnestly want them to thrive, but unless you act in ways that openly reveal the treasuring, and unless you actually do things to try and further their well-being, your love doesn't have any impact on them. The third strand of the braid is *action*, and it is here that my own framework becomes very specific, identifying the types of actions that bring about positive changes in the loved one's life.

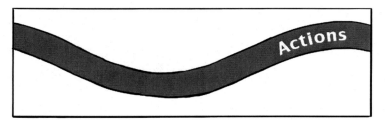

The actions that manifest devotion are ones that contribute to the ego strengths psychologist Erik Erikson identified as components of a resilient self, a self that eventually becomes capable of mutual love in adulthood and capable of taking care of the next generation and the broader community. Love that's truly worthy of the name builds up the loved one, helping them fulfill their potential as a human being, and helping them become someone capable themselves of giving love to others.

Many people think love is a complete mystery and in some ways, I agree. But as a therapist, I've had the privilege of seeing into many, many lives in addition to my own, and found some important clues that can shed light on it for you.

2

Love Builds Up, Anxiety Disrupts

Recently, I read an essay making the point that just as children learn a native language simply by hearing it all around them in early childhood, the behaviors they observe become the behavioral language they speak.[1] If shouting and arguing, physical violence, disrespecting, etc. are modeled, that's what a child will see as normal and begin to imitate.[2] If kindness, peacefulness, and respectful disagreements are the norm, that's what they expect of others and see as the goal for themselves even though moods and reactions make it challenging. To use a computer analogy, what we grew up with becomes the operating system running in the background whenever the computer is On.

If life-giving love is received and modeled, a child will feel safe. In such an interpersonal environment, they will be able to pay attention to their unique gifts and interests, developing the unique potential of their self. They will be able to do the following:

- see and hear what love looks like;
- incorporate life-enhancing interactions into their own repertoire of behaviors;
- be free to focus attention on normal developmental tasks like trying to make sense of the world around them,

figuring out how to use their bodies to maneuver in the world, learning to communicate effectively, etc.;

- be more likely to want to become someone who loves others that way; and
- be more likely to actually become someone capable of self-giving love.

On the other hand, if a child's basic physical and emotional needs are met in only minimal or chaotic ways in overwhelming, neglectful, or abusive family situations, the child's inner world will be pervaded and continually disrupted by anxiety. In this kind of environment, the mental and emotional energy that could have been used for figuring out the larger fascinating world, or could have been channeled into the blossoming of new physical and mental abilities gets siphoned off or, perhaps a better image, requisitioned and reassigned to manage that anxiety. In such a situation, the child is preoccupied with constantly monitoring the comings and goings of the person or people associated with the "I'm not safe" feelings. They are continually running an emotion radar to detect those people's arrivals and departures, gauge their moods, and get their own needs met as best they can under the circumstances. Often they form firmly fixed convictions that "I cannot trust anyone ever" and "The only person I'll ever be able to count on is me."

Danger Radar

Contrary to popular belief, it doesn't take blatant physical or sexual abuse to make an environment emotionally and psychologically unsafe and unhealthy for a child. One person in the household who infuses the home with anger or sudden disruptive unpredictability is enough. Depression in a primary caregiver is another and a very different kind of threat that creates an "I'm not safe" atmosphere for a child because it renders the caregiver largely unavailable to attune to the child's various needs. An excessively critical caregiver keeps a child on edge, continually afraid of punishment or rejection. A caregiver with chronic anxiety emits "we're not safe" messages. In this case, it's the contagious anxiety—not anything actually dangerous in the external environment—that robs the child of security. Any one of these types of disruptors is sufficient to undermine a child's optimal development and many homes have more than just one.

Creating an inner barometer for safety isn't a conscious choice the child makes. The primitive part of their brain in charge of survival simply starts doing it as soon as something wrong is perceived. This means every baby creates such a barometer since every baby experiences physical discomfort, pain, and sometimes the loneliness of not being responded to in a timely manner. Please understand that I'm not talking here about the typical frustrations and delayed gratifications that are a part of a baby having to wait their turn or deal with the normal discomforts and illnesses of childhood. Ungratified needs and wants are part of life, and good-enough parenting doesn't eliminate them altogether. Even if that were possible, it wouldn't be good for the child or anyone else since it would create unrealistic expectations of life.

Countless events can introduce anxiety into a child's environment, many of them outside the control of even the best of parents and often children themselves arrive in this world with physical conditions or temperaments that bring stress and anxiety into the home. The best a parent can do in such circumstances is be physically and emotionally available for a secure attachment to form. I'm speaking now about things parents do have some control over—in particular, themselves.

The most disruptive situation is when a parent is the trigger for a child's anxiety by being volatile, highly anxious, or depressed and unavailable. In this unfortunate situation, the person to whom the child must attach for survival is simultaneously a disruptor of the child's peace. In some cases, one parent is a cause of anxiety and the other a source of comfort, but in these situations the very fact that the disruptor continues to come and go leaves the child feeling the comforter is unwilling or unable to protect them—and so they ultimately feel unsafe. If danger is sensed continually in infancy, then before the child even leaves the starting gate of life, their way of seeing what's possible and advisable to try out in this world becomes skewed by the need to avoid the extremely uncomfortable and disruptive experience of anxiety.[3]

The Great Disrupter

In short, when there are loose cannons in a child's environment, the developing brain will use enormous amounts of mental resources for monitoring safety. Think of it this way, each of six people shipwrecked on a primitive island would be free to use all their strength and know-how to forage for food and water, make a fire, build shelter, and maybe even work on a rescue plan if they knew there were no predators on the island. But until they know they are safe, part of their attention must go toward vigilance; and if there is actual evidence of danger, their need to see an attack before it happens would distract them from those other pursuits. No one would ever feel safe to relax unless someone else was keeping watch. A child living in a home with angry, erratic, or unreliable people is on high or low alert all the time. Part of their brain is always on watch. Debra Wesselmann and her colleagues at the Attachment and Trauma Center of Nebraska have described how the survival brain takes over in children (and adults) who have had unfortunate experiences in their earliest attachment relationships. They have also developed effective team therapy to help children and their parents (biological, adoptive, or foster parents) heal from those wounds and the problem behaviors that arise from them.[4]

In order to be born—in order for the human skull to literally get through the mother's pelvic birth canal—humans are born with brains that aren't their full-size. The brain continues to increase in volume until a child is about three, all the while laying down electrical and chemical patterns that encode experience and learning. If the environment isn't emotionally and physically safe during those first three years of life during which the brain is continuing to grow new brain cells and program them for duty, that child's lifelong operating system is going to be excessively biased by one primary agenda: avoid anxiety at all costs.

Some of you reading this book were shaped by home lives in which anger or fear or depression played a huge part and I don't want you to loose heart. I want to help you understand that part of why you're having such a hard time getting it right is that your developmental path got rerouted early in life. Anxiety has a disruptive, derailing, toxic effect on a child's brain-in-the-making. It interferes with learning and it shapes relational patterns into an agenda of "do whatever it takes to lower this awful feeling." There's a good chance the personality you now live with was shaped by the lack of what Erikson called basic trust and the relative lack of freedom to develop the other ego strengths I am about to discuss.

All the communication courses in the world won't help your relationship until you begin acquiring the missing resources that can strengthen you to love more freely. Your partner may be dealing with similar deficits. While this book will not reprogram you, it may open your eyes to better understand the kind of reparative experiences you or your loved one need in order to develop the ego strengths that have remained underdeveloped. Self-understanding can lead you to seek out reprocessing therapies such as EMDR (Eye Movement Desensitization and Reprocessing), DNMS (Developmental Needs Meeting Strategy), Internal Family Systems work or neurofeedback.[5]

It's never too late.

3

The Ambivalence at the Heart of Love

I'm not sure why so little is written about this, but there is a tension at the very core of love relationships, a tension between our deep longing to be connected to that other person who has become so important to us and our strong desire to be free to do whatever we want to do whenever we want to do it. That "yes, but" is called ambivalence and unless you're prepared for it, its appearance on the scene can lead you to believe you didn't/don't love at all.

What it boils down to is that human beings tend to be pretty self-centered unless they're (1) under the influence of protective instincts, (2) in the altered brain state created by infatuation[1], or (3) they consciously and actively work against it. Even our apparent selflessness and generosity serves a deep-down desire to see ourselves as selfless—which is self-serving! When you peel away all the subtle layers to reveal what really motivates us, purely selfless love is very, very rare. (There are people who always put others ahead of themselves because they feel unworthy of equal regard. This is a subtle and well-camouflaged preoccupation with self, far too complex to address here.)

Ambivalence about attachment, if not openly apparent, is often just beneath the surface. Parents love their children and yet sometimes feel trapped by the responsibility of having them. Committed couples want the advantages of coupledom, but feel strangled and suffocated by the limits it puts on their personal freedom at times. Being there for a good friend when they need you sometimes means saying no to something you'd been looking forward to doing. It's at the core of human nature, this ambivalence about connectedness and separateness. It starts with our earliest attachments in childhood and though it may fade, it doesn't fully go away. Throughout most of life, we all secretly or openly want attachment on our own terms. We come down on different sides of the ambivalence at different times, depending on the particular relationship and on our mood.

The longing to be thoroughly connected when you want it, but separate enough to be free when you want that instead is behind the initiative vs. guilt dilemma Erikson noted in the third stage of development. It is a dilemma I've learned more about from the work of another psychologist, Margaret Mahler, and from life experience—personal and with clients. For one thing, I've learned that it cuts both ways: the toddler is ambivalent about separating and most mothers are ambivalent about losing the intimate dependency that has, at times, felt suffocating. The guilt is complex: If the mom isn't ready to let go when the child wants to do so, her nonverbal and sometimes verbal messages foster guilt feelings in the child for venturing forth into life as their own center of gravity. If the mom is ready and the child isn't, the mom may feel guilt for wanting back some of her former breathing room. And if they're both ready, the mom may still feel guilty for being so relieved the child is prospering on their own.

The dilemma brought about by natural growth and development in the child is simultaneously interpersonal and intrapsychic. This duality is true of all the developmental crises or conflicts Erikson described. (He uses *crisis* in the sense of *the perfect storm*—the convergence of physical, psychological, and social developments that bring an issue to a head.) It takes place privately inside each person's heart/mind and openly in the dance of how the two people interact. It's the complexity of this attachment-separation ambivalence that keeps our unfinished business with parents playing itself out over and over again in our adult relationships. Behind the masks of adults in many marital tensions, there's often a two- or three-year-old or an adolescent reliving attachment-separation problems from long ago, experiencing the spouse as a stand-in for the parent in the earlier dynamics. When both spouses have unfinished business from their pasts, things can heat up very quickly with neither one maturely responding to present-day data.

Even in today's divorce-prevalent world, couples "in love" get so caught up in the exquisite and intense and often painful experience of connectedness that they temporarily forget and minimize how important doing their own thing has been in life up until that point in time. And they are blind to the fact that it will probably (dare I say "definitely"?) become important to them again. Most premarital counselors and ministers tell couples some version of "the honeymoon will end and that's when learning to love each other really starts," but few counselees download that bit of data. Who wants that kind of rain on their parade? The truth is that because some version of the pattern has happened at least twice before in each of their lives—in early childhood and in adolescence—couples are prone to react strongly when the ambivalence emerges in their relationship. It's all too common for couples to complain that their spouse is "acting just like my father" or "just like my mother."

The unvarnished truth is this: Every one of us has our very own little (or large) monster of self-centeredness, and if we marry, we bring it with us. It may have gone into hibernation during courtship, but it is sure to reawaken. Survival as a couple depends on whether both individuals want a good relationship enough to tame and train their monsters.

I want to help you understand and make peace with this ambivalence about attachment so you can become more comfortable working with it openly in your relationships. Ignorance about it breeds misunderstandings which undermine trust, so you'll have a better chance of loving well in adulthood if you see these dynamics more clearly and try not to take them so personally. Figuring out how to be securely attached and comfortably separate is a task in every marriage. Margaret Mahler's insight into what she called the psychological birth of the human infant gave me the template that has allowed me to better understand some of the relational tensions in adolescence and in marriage, so I'll begin by describing what she saw happening between birth and around age three.

First Time Through the Spiral: Early Childhood

Mahler and her graduate students closely observed the interactions between mothers and their babies up to kindergarten age. Their research took place in the 1950s, a time when most children were nurtured by their mothers during their preschool years, and I can only tell you that even in the age of early daycare, I still see evidence of the same dynamics playing out. Whatever your position on the daycare debates if you have one, I ask you to set it aside at least temporarily.[2] The attachment-separation dynamics Mahler observed are relevant to loving well, whatever your childcare arrangements.

Overly simplified, she saw that when the parenting is good enough, a child forms a secure attachment in the first five months or so and then begins to *hatch*—a word I've always found wonderfully whimsical. With its imagery of a tiny creature breaking out of an egg into the larger world, she captures the way babies' mental and physical development allows them to start experiencing the world around them. The ability to sit up on their own is the beginning, followed by crawling and then toddling—ever-improving the position from which to observe their surroundings. You can see their brain taking in all the data from their senses. Hatching out of the psychological womb of a secure emotional bond, the child begins to experience their separateness. Mahler called the whole experience separation/individuation to emphasize that over the course of many, many months an externally observable reality (the physical ability to come and go under their own steam) is taking place simultaneously with an internal invisible realization (I am a self/individual different from you) that is both exciting and somewhat frightening.

Hatching gives way to *practicing* as the brain and muscle maturation take place. The child actively practices using their body's ability to make things happen and mentally process everything their senses take in. Mahler noted this period of happily exploring and practicing takes place from roughly nine months to sixteen months, a time during which the child delights in sharing their discoveries with the primary attachment figure, usually the mother. The practicing produces increasing evidence that what's going on inside them and what's going on inside mom is different, something that's utterly obvious to any older observer, but which comes as a disturbing revelation in the mental and emotional development of a toddler.

Around eighteen months for most toddlers, an internal struggle begins, a struggle that will escalate and lasts about a year. Parents know it as *the terrible twos* since it is so filled with interpersonal struggles and individual meltdowns. Mahler picked a rather unwieldy term for this important phase—rapprochement. It's French and in international relations it means the reestablishment of cordial relations after a time of tension or open conflict. The terrible twos are filled with push-pull, dig-in-my-heels, stubborn-but-still-needy behaviors that are extremely difficult for parents to handle. Most parents would readily acknowledge that "tension and open conflict" accurately describe that stretch of time. So Mahler's choice of words captures the forecast of peaceful resolution as well as the universal upheaval.

As we will see in the next chapter, Erikson describes the stage as dominated by working out whether it's okay/safe/acceptable to take initiative and pursue one's own purposes.

Erikson based his theory primarily on what he had learned from working with adults who were trying to sort out retrospectively where their problems had come from. In contrast, Mahler and her assistants closely observed infants and mothers from birth right on through this crunch time. Her theory captures the child's obvious and strong ambivalence about being dependent, attached, and embedded in relationship. With emerging physical and cognitive abilities, a child this age desperately wants to prove they can "do it myself!" They alternate between feeling filled with bravery and confidence and then feeling overwhelmed by what they've taken on, so they run back to the safe home base of mommy (or whoever they're attached to—hopefully there is someone) and get emotionally refueled by that person's presence and availability.

Mahler observed in child after child that the tension seemed to come to a head somewhere between eighteen and twenty-two months—the rapprochement crisis—and if the parenting is steady enough, the child then settles down and reattaches in a different way, a way that seems to be based on a more advanced awareness of having a separate self and a new comfort level with that reality. If things go well enough, cordial relations are reestablished and the child's mental, emotional, psychological, and physical energies are freed up to be devoted to the development of new competencies in various arenas as childhood progresses. As we will see in the next chapter, this allows all the ego strengths to continue functioning as resources toward the eventual crystallization of a sense of self-identity during adolescence and early adulthood. If anxiety is a major factor in the child's world, they may not experience permission to continue exploring and discovering their unique interests and abilities, but instead become overly compliant in ways that lead to an increasingly false self. Optimally, the child's nurturers are able to discipline the willfulness while still encouraging creative exploration of the self's potentials—harder to do with some children than others.

Here's what it looks like the first time through the attachment-separation spiral:

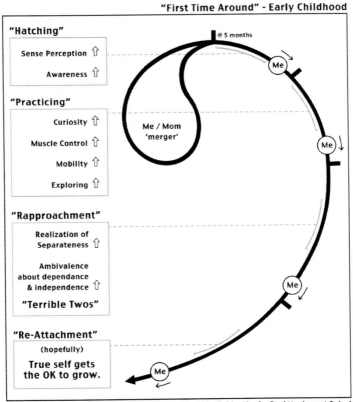

The Attachment > [Separation / Individuation] > Re-Attachment Spiral
(Adapted from the work of Margaret Mahler)

Second Time Through the Spiral: Adolescence

The push-pull of adolescence and launching as a young adult has a lot of similarities to the psychological birth sequence. Picture MapQuest or Google Maps or the weather maps on the

Internet where you can focus in on a city block or zoom out and see the whole city, or zoom out further and see the whole continent. If we zoom out from the early childhood spiral and let childhood itself become the center of the spiral, we see the same pattern of close attachment, separation, and (hopefully) reattachment taking place on a longer scale between birth and young adulthood.

So let's zoom out from the self from birth till three and look at the self from birth till about twenty-five. Now it's home and family that's the egg and hatching comes about due to the biological/sexual changes of puberty and the cognitive developments around age twelve that make abstract thinking possible. These two developments create and propel a breakout into the wider world beyond childhood. (Many would say today's media breaks the shell considerably before the creature inside stops needing its protection. It may be that exposure from a young age to television and movies meant for older audiences may keep the shell from adequately forming in the first place.)

As most readers will remember all too well, the years of adolescence are their own prolonged period of ambivalence about having to (still) be dependent. Embedded in the family and its rules and controls, dependent on parents for sustenance and support, forced to accept confrontive and tough love at times, adolescents are in a love-hate relationship with their parents to varying degrees. They want the benefits of attachment, but they *don't* want the controls or limits inherent in family life and many resist the responsible participation expected of them as they get older.

In many cultures, there are formal rites of passage that coincide with adolescent hatching, after which the teenager is recognized as being an adult-in-training. They are expected to practice bearing adult responsibilities and roles for a number of years before being ready to manage on their own. Modern Western culture since WWII has postponed the age at which teens are expected to bear full adult responsibilities, holding out college as the widespread norm. As a result, North American teens spend many years in the ambiguous status of "no longer a child but not yet a self-sustaining and fully independent" adult. Erikson is most widely known for his writings on the identity search that takes place during these years.

Just as children in the rapprochement phase are angry at not being big enough to do all the things big kids can do, teens often become angry at not yet being allowed to exercise the adult freedoms for which they feel ready and to which they feel entitled. They may love their parents, but they also resent still being dependent on them and having to answer to them. It's fairly common for the resulting power struggle to produce crises of various kinds. Eventually, if things go well enough, they launch successfully from the family nest and become able to support themselves, perhaps starting a new family. It's only then, having become largely self-sustaining and separate, that they can fully experience the satisfaction of reattaching to their family of origin on the new grounds of having a more fully solidifying adult identity.

Launching from the family and becoming self-sustaining allows a person to reattach to their parents as an adult whose separateness they recognize and whom they respect as an individual in their own right. If parents have loved well enough via the Nurture Loves and Challenge Loves, their adult children are more likely to want to reattach to them in a new way as adults.

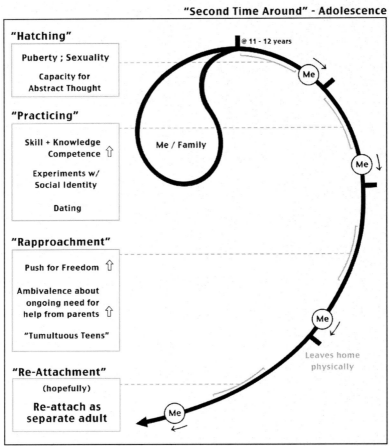

The Attachment > [Separation / Individuation] > Re-Attachment Spiral
(Adapted from the work of Margaret Mahler)

Another Time Around the Spiral: Adult Romance

It should come as no surprise, really, that this by-now familiar ambivalence about attachment usually shows up again when two adults try to figure out how to be married. People call it *getting hitched* for good reason: it's confining. Falling in love and becoming attached tends to be the easy part. That's the center of the spiral this time, the adult experience of psychological merger, the "I can't live without you" self-created cocoon in which earlier friendships with others fall by the wayside as the couple disappears into an all-consuming preoccupation with each other. I'll talk more about the physiology of in loveness when I describe cherishing in chapter 6, but for now let's just acknowledge that during this phase of a relationship, the two people feel so much a part of each other that they have a hard time thinking of themselves as separate.

"No really, honey, I'd enjoy a bike ride. The guys can tell me about the game later."

If a commitment is made[3], there comes a time somewhere down the road—generally by the end of the second year if not sooner—when "the honeymoon is over." Older couples nod knowingly when they hear about the big fight or the flight home to mom and dad; they knew this day would come. Why? Because as I pointed out at the beginning of this chapter, people don't remain in that state of selflessness they experienced in the cocoon. They just don't. Once they've been together for a while, the brain chemistry begins returning to its former state and they begin to hatch out of the cocoon just as surely as the five-month-old and the eleven-year-old did.

When the brain stops pumping out the selfishness-suppressing chemicals, the pre-in-love person resurfaces with all their lifelong interests, preferences, quirks, habits, etc. Those may have been evident all along or they may have been muted to a great extent. My students don't like to hear this, but I advise them to be sure they know who that person they're living with was before they met since that's likely the person who's going to reappear at some point in the not-too-distant future.

Rapprochement dynamics happen again as both people inevitably start asserting their separate wants (or at least they'd like to) and the fate of the marriage depends on whether they learn how to love each other in spite of their differences. In other words, can their relationship survive when each wakes up from the illusion of being perfectly fine with continual self-sacrifice? Either they practice learning more about each other and figure out how to take each other into account, or they simply start asserting their wills. Not surprisingly, when there is push back, many couples complain that a spouse is treating them just like their mother or father did. The experience of having their separateness restrained or channeled or stifled is a very familiar one, after all, since they've been through this experience before at least twice!

The version of practicing during this adult experience of the spiral involves learning what it really means to be devoted to another person, allowing them to count just as much as you count. In one sense, the rest of a lifelong marriage is the rapprochement phase because truth be told, we never get over our ambivalence about losing the freedom to just do what we feel like doing. A child can't choose to leave. Adolescents can't legally choose to leave their parents until sixteen and it's not usually feasible until eighteen or older. But adults in a relationship are free to throw in the towel and walk away.

It's not widely known that learning how to be married means learning how to accommodate the need for separateness within a secure attachment. The exercise of individual autonomy and willpower, individual initiative and pursuit of purposes, diligence and the acquisition of individual competencies—the ego strengths Erikson identified—need to be given a place within the shared identity of marriage. This takes practice. There will be rocky times. There will be what the Gottmans call "regrettable incidents" where you blow it. Only if you both commit to the habit of taking each other into account and the habit of reestablishing cordial relations through apologies and forgiveness when either of you blows it will you learn how to be married.

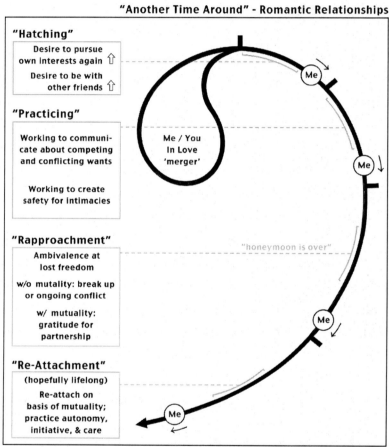

The Attachment > [Separation / Individuation] > Re-Attachment Spiral
(Adapted from the work of Margaret Mahler)

Part 2:
The Goal of Love—
Love Builds Up

4

The Components of a Resilient Self

The idea of self-esteem has been beaten into the ground so much in the last couple of decades that many people are tired of hearing about it. If your self-esteem is low or nonexisting, you feel defeated and if you have someone with low self-esteem in your life, you may be weary of seeing and hearing about how hard life is for them. But I can't share what I know about love without talking about the components of a solid sense of self. If you have them, appropriate self-esteem follows naturally.

Many writers have used the image of a container of some sort inside a person to convey the experience of being empty or full of good feelings about the self. A water tank, a cistern, a fuel tank, a canteen, a water bottle—each image has its own points to recommend it. I like the portability of the water bottle and canteen images, and how easily we relate to the idea of getting thirsty and needing our bottles refilled. But I can't seem to get away from how readily "love tank" comes to my mind and out of my mouth when I talk to clients. So picture a water tank in your chest when you're born. It's part of the original equipment and it needs to be filled up immediately upon arrival. If a child is cared for in ways that convey they matter to their parents, liquid is poured into the tank. I think of it as water for the journey of life. The first deposits into a person's self-esteem tank come from the outside—from their caregivers. Once language forms, how people feel about themselves is a direct result of how they think about themselves, but long before words can be understood or spoken, it's the nonverbal messages that convey everything. A parent's presence or absence, how quickly or slowly they respond if they do respond, the positive or negative energy they give off (their mood), their tone of voice, whether they handle the baby gently or roughly—all of these nonverbals convey messages to the infant. I think of every person as having a Matter Meter inside them, calibrated to pick up data about whether they're important to the people significant to them, and that meter doesn't go away when we grow up.

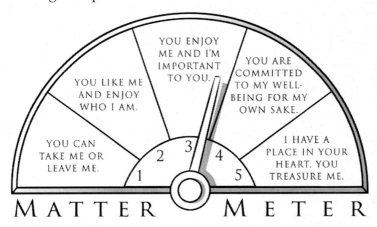

In part 4, you'll read about the kinds of actions that let a person know they matter to you. For now, I'll just say that mattering is a very important initial source of self-worth for any child. As you read more about the ego strengths, you'll understand that having their autonomy and initiative affirmed also pours supplies into their tank. Having their competencies recognized by the people who matter to them also adds water. As a person matures, they often become able to take appropriate pride in their own accomplishments and value as a person, adding water even if others are unaware.

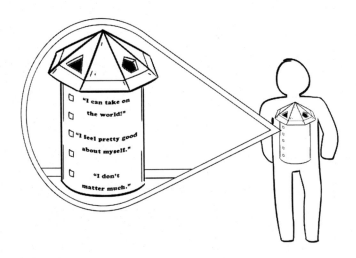

Unfortunately, if a person internalizes negative messages about their worth or acceptability in childhood, it's as if the intake valves all get closed tightly. Picture a lid with cutout openings that only allow certain kinds of evidence or affirmation from certain people to get in—like a toddler's hollow toy for learning shapes. That can really undermine a person's development of self-esteem. I'll talk more about this in part 4.

Esteeming/valuing/regarding yourself appropriately is another way of talking about self-love. Each of us is born with potentials we can develop and share with the world, and there is a natural sense of satisfaction and fulfillment that accompanies doing so. The single greatest potential any and everyone of us has is the potential to love. Treasuring is not reduced by intellect or limited by material wealth. With a loving attitude and knowledge of how to show that love effectively, each of us can affect the world in ways that multiply exponentially.

Healthy self-love (not arrogance or self-centered entitlement) is essential to a healthy loving relationship with someone else. You can't love another person well if you're giving yourself preferential treatment, and you can't love the other person well if you don't reveal your own needs and wants in a manner that lets them take you into account. The foundation of relational love between adults is what Erikson calls *mutuality*. Other ways of talking about it include:

- taking each other into account;
- treating others as you'd like to be treated;
- not treating people in ways you wouldn't want to be treated; and
- loving your neighbor—your fellow human being, that is—with as much concern as you love yourself.

Although many religious and philosophical systems teach mutual love, promote it, and even command it, it's not very easy to actually do it. Not over the long haul. Unfortunately, for some reason, it's especially hard to do with the people we live in closest quarters with—our spouses and families.

Erik Erikson wrote a lot of articles and books in the 1960s and '70s to explain the developmental stages he first presented in 1959. His psychological language can get in the way, so I'm going to oversimplify the theory to help explain how a person ideally accumulates the building blocks (ingredients/components/tools) needed to have a reasonably well-functioning adult personality. He called these *ego strengths* and said they develop well or poorly as a child-teen-young adult grows physically and mentally within the context of interpersonal feedback and input from the important people in their life. I'll be using a variety of visual images as I go along to help get Erikson's insights across and, hopefully, at least some of them will click for you.

Some of my students have been skeptical of Erikson's presentation of the ideal, observing that "nobody's life is really like that so how can anyone turn out okay?" Like many of my clients, some of them grew up in situations that gave them few clues—and sometimes many misleading ones—about love. My response is that a person needs to know what the goal looks like before they can recognize it or hope to come close to reaching it.

I want to be clear that I am using Erikson's general framework as the scaffolding on which to build my more encompassing way of thinking about love. The only ideas from his work that have really made it into the general public's thinking have to do with adolescents being on an identity search and even that is only cliché. His primary contribution to developmental psychology is known as a stage theory and once people have studied Erikson in psychology classes, they can't seem to get away from the image of discrete layers—implying that each ego strength belongs to a particular layer or floor in the ever-growing-taller building. It wasn't until I had started raising my own children and been a therapist for about fifteen years that I began to really understand how the opportunity to begin developing one particular ego strength such as autonomy/willpower may first show up around two (which is why Erikson makes it the central building block of his second stage), but it's always hovering around the edges or may again take center stage at any time throughout the rest of life. And the capacity or need to engage in another strength such as generativity/care may not be full-blown until adulthood, but is often practiced in fledgling ways much earlier in life, for instance by a child playing house or by a young teen babysitting or volunteering at a hospital or nursing home. I hope by the time you finish reading this book, you'll understand that the issues and opportunities of each so-called stage permeate life.

It also took living several decades with family, friends, and clients for me to really understand that regardless of a person's chronological age, they continue to thrive best when the people around them support their appropriate exercise of autonomy, pursuit of purposes, and their acquisition of new competencies. Unbeknownst to us, some of the adults around us are trying secretly to acquire some of these ego strengths for the first time or to bolster shaky ones while other people are simply negotiating for chances to fit their wants together with the wants of other people. Loving others well means finding ways to support their initial acquisition, remedial acquisition, and/or reasonable exercise of ego strengths throughout life.

My own college and early-adult reading of Erikson also failed to recognize how differently the eight ego strengths function in his theory (and more importantly, in life). His best-known writings present the ego strengths of adulthood as if they were similar to those of childhood and adolescence, but it's more accurate to say that when certain internal resources are nurtured early in life, they can eventually consolidate into a strong self and then bear fruit in adulthood. In other words, it is optimal for the first four, listed below, to develop during childhood:

- trust/hope/faith;
- autonomy/willpower;
- initiative/purpose; and
- industry (diligence)/competencies.

These are the prime ingredients or building blocks needed to help a person crystallize a self/identity during adolescence and young adulthood, the task of Erikson's fifth stage. The last three stages identified by Erikson are the following:

- intimacy/mutuality;
- generativity/care; and
- integrity/wisdom.

These are the outcomes or capacities of someone with a sufficient supply of the first four and a solid sense of self. I apologize for the multiple words for each of the ego strengths. Erikson's original writings use a variety of words to capture what he's getting at, and I've found it does take more than one to convey each of the rich inner resources he's identifying.

It's important to understand fully what these inner resources are so as I describe them, I'll give some examples. I have put an abbreviated explanation of Erikson in Appendix A.

Erikson's Developmental Theory

Each ego strength a person develops becomes a resource that helps them more successfully develop and use the next ones. Like basic tools added to a toolbox, they make it easier to do the next developmental tasks as they come along. For instance, a child who is adequately sustained will stay alive and grow physically whether hope is planted at their psychological core or not, but when trust and hope are there, the child faces the next opportunities and challenges of life with greater confidence and resilience. Because the world around them will present new challenges and expectations based on their physical size and chronological age, they will be at a distinct disadvantage if they haven't acquired the assets to meet those challenges. Kindergarten and elementary school teachers are accustomed to having to accommodate the wide age ranges during which mental and emotional skills develop in young children, but the physical march to adulthood continues whether the tools are accumulated or not. Rightly or wrongly, once an individual has left high school, the surrounding world tends to assume that an emotionally and psychologically mature person lives inside that adult body. For instance, an employer sees a middle-aged woman at the workstation in front of them and assumes she has a reasonable amount of autonomy and initiative to back up certain competencies evident in her resume. If her job performance doesn't bear that out, she may retain her job, but she's not likely to be promoted and may not understand why not.

It's not unlike math. If you try to tackle higher math when you didn't learn adding and multiplying earlier, you're less likely to breeze through the challenges of algebra. And then a weak grasp of algebra puts you at a disadvantage if you're in a situation where geometry is called for. It's not impossible to go back and acquire or shore up the shaky basics—obviously the best solution. More often, just as people try with varying degrees of success to mask the holes in their education, people with minimal trust, autonomy, or initiative live with a dread of having their deficiencies show, of being found out. Many forms of therapy are, in essence, remedial parenting to help a person develop or strengthen these resources.

It's also the case that even if a person gets a good start on each of the ego strengths in childhood, the middle school years and puberty bring on a new hatching that can make a teenager almost as psychologically vulnerable as a baby. It's not uncommon for ego strengths developed later in life such as various adulthood competencies to hide mistrust or self-doubt lingering from childhood or adolescence.

I doubt that any of us are ever truly finished developing and bolstering these components of a resilient self; therefore, it's a mistake to picture discrete, contained stages as if that floor is over and done with while the next floor is built on top of it. Storms come along throughout life, stirring up old unfinished business and revealing the need to shore up pilings whose weakness wasn't evident when the weather was clear.

Stage 1: Trust vs. Mistrust:
Components to Begin Adding: Basic Trust/Hope/Faith

In the first year of life, a baby is completely at the mercy of bigger people to keep them alive. If someone meets their survival needs for safety, food and water, and sufficient clothing and shelter, they will probably live long enough for their brain to mature and start making sense out of the world around them. How well someone meets those survival needs and how secure the baby feels emotionally around that person or people tells the baby whether the world is trustworthy. If the child's physical needs are met in a fairly dependable way and if they are cared for by someone who tunes in sufficiently and allows an attachment to form with them, the sense of being welcomed and safe in that first year plants a seed of hope at the core of the child's personality. The basic trust and hope become resources for life, tools that will make them braver as their physical body grows and their brain becomes capable of directing its movements.

Psychologists who have followed in the line of thinking of Harry Stack Sullivan[1] have long recognized that a person's need to feel safe and secure dominates and shapes how they go about everything else in life. It will influence how they approach school, extracurricular activities, job searches, and how genuine and self-revealing they are as they seek friends and a mate. Having a core of hopefulness about life is like the rubber or cork core at the center of a baseball—it gives resilience (bounce) in the face of hardship or setbacks.

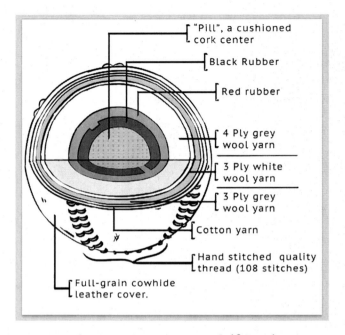

Stage 2: Autonomy vs. Self-Doubt:
Continue Strengthening Trust/Hope/Faith
Components to add: Autonomy/Willpower

Regardless of whether the baby feels psychologically safe or not, their growing body and brain will propel them into self-willed motion and their mind will busily try to organize what they are experiencing and make sense of it. The baby constantly monitors the facial expressions, tone of voice, and body language of whoever takes care of them, looking for clues about whether they are okay in that person's eyes. Psychologists speak of this process as *mirroring* and it's an important concept to understand.

Mirroring

You and I know the difference between our image seen in a normal mirror, what we see in a fun house mirror that has built-in distortions, and being shown a photograph of ourselves. You and I pretty much know that a normal mirror doesn't lie. If you look into a mirror and see a smudge on your cheek, you're probably going to try to clean off your cheek. If you look in a mirror and your face appears clean, you're not going to reach for a washcloth. If you go to a carnival and walk past a mirror that makes you look fifteen-feet tall and curved in weird ways, you know the mirror is lying and you laugh; you don't suddenly think you need to go buy a new wardrobe to fit this strange new body. You know the reflection is not an accurate picture of you.

The mind of a child is not nearly as sophisticated as yours and mine. For one thing, a baby's experience of the world is confined only to what's happening right here, right this minute, within the range their senses can grasp. What a baby can see, hear, smell, taste, or touch is all that exists as far as their mind is concerned at this age. There's no ability to know that you, the nurturer, continue to exist somewhere else if you're not within visual or hearing range. Similarly, for a young child the caregivers' facial expression, tone of voice, body language, and eventually their words when around the child function as mirrors, showing the baby/child what they interpret as an accurate reflection of their own value or worth. Everything they see is metabolized as being about them. When a baby sees tenderness and joy on the face of their parent or caregiver and hears it in their voice, the baby sees, hears, and believes "I'm wonderful. I give joy." When a baby sees tension, anger, or distress on the face and in the voice and manner of being of the parent or caregiver, the baby sees, hears, and believes "I'm a problem. There's something wrong with me."

The baby's brain is not sophisticated enough yet to know of events beyond the immediate environment. The anger that's actually at your spouse tells the baby (erroneously but absolutely) that *they* have been bad somehow. The sadness that's actually about your best friend moving away tells the baby (erroneously but absolutely) that *they* have been disappointing to you in some way. The circumstances going on in your wider world have no meaning to them because they don't exist for the child. Their mind has no place for absent realities yet. Their caregivers are the

Carol J. Sherman, PhD

world for them and they look into their faces and absorb their calmness or stress to discover whether or not *they* are an okay person and whether or not they are safe.

This is really important to understand, so I'm going to make it personal. Imagine that when you were eighteen months old, everybody watching you and your family from outside the circle knew the negativity in the air wasn't primarily about you—it was because of a favorite uncle's terminal cancer diagnosis right on the heels of your dad's car accident and disability. And your big brother's ADHD problems at school weren't helping the mood around the house either. But for you, inside the circle and aware of only what was taking place inside the circle, it was all about you. And in your implicit memory system[2], before you had words for what was happening, you probably internalized all of that uncertainty and confusion as "the world is unsafe" and also as "there's something wrong with me." It's not in verbal language you can retrieve, but it's there programmed into your brain's neurological patterns that get activated again by various life situations. These irrational core beliefs block water intake into your tank. For reasons that make absolutely no sense at all to the adult you or to the people around you now (people who see all the evidence of your gifts and abilities and positive presence in the world), you remain filled with self-doubt instead of willpower and self-confidence based on your obvious competencies.

The power of mirroring to shape or misshape a child's self-image is captured well in the film version of *The Help* in a scene where the African-American maid Abilene (who is also the *de facto* nanny for the white child in the home) has repeatedly seen and heard the mother treat the child dismissively out of her own meanness and self-centeredness. Sensitive to the mistreatment, Abilene has found private times to look directly into the child's eyes and give her an unmistakable accurate message about herself: "You are kind. You are smart. You are important." At the end of the film, when Abilene has been fired on trumped-up charges, before leaving the home, she makes sure to give the child one last dose of the affirming message she has tried to instill in her, asking the little girl to say out loud to her: "I am kind. I am smart. I am important."[3]

Remember the analogy to the fun house mirrors. It's important to recognize that the information a child gets from their parents' behavior when around them, as well as their parents' responses directly to them, are experienced by that child as accurately reflecting the child's being and worth. The truth you and I know about all the other things that affect parents' lives doesn't keep the child from seeing a smudge where there really isn't one. (Conversely, it's also true that if the child has an actual disability of some kind—the equivalent of a smudge—and the parents' love minimizes its importance, it will not dominate the child's self-image as much as it otherwise might.)

Grasping this concept of mirroring is extremely important for understanding why the primary attachment figures and caregivers have such an impact on a child's development of the ego strengths Erikson identified.[4]

And Now Back to Stage 2

Long before actual words convey meaning to them, children interpret their caregiver's reactions as reward and punishment, affirmation or rejection. They begin censoring the expression of the true self this early in life. In one sense, it's simply the process whereby a child becomes civilized. The people raising the child are sometimes guided by their culture's expectations (for instance, how children are potty trained in the US culture is very different from what toddlers in third world villages are taught), and at other times, parental figures are instilling idiosyncratic expectations such as never ever to touch objects on the side tables.

Sometimes the seeds of self-doubt are planted by the arrival of another child when a person-in-the-making is a toddler. It's a natural event people tend to report in retrospect as *no big deal* and on one hand, they're right. But on the other hand, the timing of a new sibling can have a significant impact on a child's sense of self-worth, and how the toddler is handled by key adults at that time makes a huge difference. Just this week, a middle-aged client spoke of how surprised her now-adult daughter was by how much she had enjoyed collaborating with her younger brother on planning a family celebration. "I have no idea why I hated him so much throughout our childhood," her daughter had told her after the event. My client, however, recalled clearly that the pregnancy with her son had been a difficult one, reducing her time with her then-toddler daughter; the baby brother's vulnerable health had a prolonged impact on mom's emotional and physical availability to this daughter. The resentment made complete sense to my client who felt badly that her daughter had been displaced, but there had been little she could have done differently at the time.

Psychologist Heinz Kohut focused attention on the ups and downs of healthy self-love, "the good kind of narcissism"—a phrase many people erroneously think is a self-contradiction.[5] Kohut traced many of his clients' self-disorders back to two key needs that weren't met well enough in early life:

- the normal need to experience being the center of someone's world for at least a short while in the first year or so, and
- the need to have that grandiose illusion gradually fade as the mother's attention focuses elsewhere, which ideally happens at about the same time the toddler's enjoyment of the larger world is making mom less essential to their sense of well-being. In other words, as the toddler's mind gets more and more interested in what's going on with other people and in mastering new tasks (in Mahler's template, individuation is well underway), it's not such a blow to their heart that mommy loves other people and enjoys doing other things, too. If the basic trust and budding autonomy are there, the child can incorporate

this knowledge without being plunged into lasting self-doubt.

Many problems people experience with their sense of selfhood, said Kohut, have their roots in (1) never having experienced even the short period of specialness children need in infancy and toddlerhood; (2) being abruptly ejected from feeling special rather than having the illusion diminish gradually; and (3) having the specialness prolong into a way of life, creating a sense of entitlement to it (what we used to call being spoiled). Common usage of the term *narcissist* links it only to this third circumstance (i.e., someone who arrogantly acts entitled to having the rest of the world exist for his or her own personal agenda).

What few people realize is that while this attitude can result from having been allowed to continue ruling the roost in the family well beyond the healthy temporary specialness in toddlerhood, it can also be a compensatory reaction to being disillusioned abruptly rather than gradually. In these cases, there is a deep core of self-doubt behind the "I'm the center of the world" façade and very often the adult has no conscious memory of the wound because it lives on in the implicit, but not the explicit memory. Whether it's displacement by a rival sibling, loss due to divorcing parents, the death of a caregiver, or something else, anger often competes with pain inside the mind and heart of the child. If anger dominates, it can come out as demands and entitlement. If pain and sadness dominate, it can come out as withdrawal or depression. Either way, in these cases, the self-doubt of "I'm not good enough" sends its root down deeper into the soil and trust and hope, to whatever extent they were there, are shaken.

> Todd came home after going to the Midwest to attend his sister's wedding. Becky had been a single mom for two years and was now marrying a man she had been living with for the previous year. With sadness, Todd described how his toddler niece would run into the room and try to climb into her mom's lap. Becky played video games pretty

constantly when she was at home and typically pushed her daughter away, saying "Go play with your toys. I didn't want you anyway." Todd tried to give his niece some attention while he was there, but he knew his tiny drop of positive attention was going into a mostly empty love tank.

On the other hand, when things go relatively well, a toddler's attachment figures (Parents? Nanny? Grandparent? Whoever is present enough physically and emotionally for the child to bond with) do treasure them and convey that they are welcome and safe. These adults make the environment safe enough that most of the time they can allow the child to go ahead and exercise willpower through reaching and kicking, exploring safe objects, then by crawling and eventually by walking. Of course there are limits, but for the most part, the child receives the message that their explorations and efforts are acceptable and good and that they are pretty wonderful just because they exist and are doing what toddlers naturally do. If this happens, autonomy and a budding experience of willpower become tools in their toolbox for building a life.

An inner sense of autonomy is like having a force within you that you can exert for making things happen. As a child, making a Big Wheel teardown the sidewalk by the force of their own legs captures it well. Or picture a huge, heavy crate blocking your path and you lean your whole weight into it and by sheer force of the energy within you and your will to do it, you move it out of the way. It's also exerting yourself to follow through on a training program to run a marathon, or asserting yourself to risk traveling in a foreign country. It's the experience of empowerment to get something done and it's needed to turn the next stage's budding possibility—initiative—into reality.

It is enormously challenging for parents to discipline their small children and set limits on bad behavior without squashing their uniqueness. A client recently expressed her gratitude for how consistent her mother had been in separating the unacceptable behavior from the acceptable and loved child. It should be a goal for every parent.

Stage 3: Initiative vs. Guilt Continue Strengthening Trust/Hope/Faith and Autonomy/Willpower Components to Add: Initiative/(In Pursuit of) Purpose

Erikson calls the next tool initiative and the ego strength a child will hopefully develop is the ability to pursue a purpose without feeling guilty about it. In chapter 3, I discussed this material more fully in the larger context of attachments throughout life, but it's important to present it carefully here in its proper developmental place as well. As explained earlier I've come to understand this stage and what's at stake by bringing Erikson into conversation with Margaret Mahler who focused closely and carefully on the preschool years. She was interested in what she called *the psychological birth* of a human infant, an image that requires us to visualize a new metaphor: the baby's psychological/emotional bond with their mother is the womb in which their sense of self continues to gestate after physical birth. A baby's first weeks are largely autistic, fading in and out of sleep as their body recovers from physical birth and adjusts to processing food and air. If all goes well, the baby bonds securely with one person in particular and then begins only gradually, as they are able to tolerate it emotionally, to experience the evidence that they are separate.

We know that forming a secure attachment to someone is what gives a child a strong foundation. Speculation abounds on both sides of debates about early daycare and much research is being carried out to assess how the widespread changes in child-rearing of the last decades will affect the attachment-separation process. Rather than get sidetracked by this highly charged emotional subject, let's operate on the hope that an infant/toddler can feel securely attached to a parent who spends quality time with them each morning, at night, and on weekends and holidays. In Mahler's close observation of babies, toddlers, and their mothers (her research was in the 1950s), she paid careful attention to how the mothers responded to their child's tentative or bold moves to do things on their own. Bottom line: Did the mom encourage the baby's initiative in exploring and trying out new things as they became physically able and intellectually curious or did she discourage them from doing so?

All parents—at least if they're paying attention—will call a child back from actual danger or physically intervene to keep them safe, which often seems very black and white, but parents differ greatly about the gray area as a child tries out new abilities and tests their own limits. There is a wide range of how mothers/nurturers handle the evidence that their child is growing up and needs her less. Some encourage it, either because they enjoy seeing the growth or because they're eager for their own increased freedom. Others are sad to see it, knowing it spells the end of a phase they have enjoyed. Many are ambivalent and hide it; others are ambivalent and show it. Small children have sensors that detect the messages about this as well as other signs of whether or not they are acceptable.[6] Sometimes they interpret accurately and sometimes they misinterpret.

You Matter to Me

One of the most predictable disagreements between mothers and fathers concerns how much risk to allow their toddler, child, or teen to take as they grow up. To some extent, this is about encouraging autonomy, but at another level, it's about whether it's okay to go off and do things separately "from me." Neurological research shows that the male brain is much more inclined to see risk-taking behavior as a natural and good part of life and as contributing to self-esteem. The average female brain doesn't get the same kind of neurological payoff from thrill-seeking. Research reveals that risk-taking and tolerance of it in others seems to be connected with testosterone. Since fathers tend to become more involved as their children become more active, it follows that children tend to receive more encouragement from their fathers for initiatives that show "I'm separate from you. I'm growing up" as well as for initiatives that may seem a bit risky in a mom's eyes.

To sum up where we are so far, if a child has a good amount of basic trust in the relationship as a safety net, they approach life with hopefulness as a toddler. And that hope and trust give them ballast as they start sailing in the boat that is becoming their self. If they are encouraged to use their newly emerging physical abilities and to explore with their newly crystallizing mental curiosity, they start feeling like there's an autonomous center of gravity inside them. And if they then get the message that they can become more ambitious without jeopardizing the close relationship(s) that has given them the security in the first place, they start feeling good about taking initiative and pursuing purposes that originate in their own mind.

If, on the other hand, they get verbal and nonverbal messages that the person on whom they are most dependent emotionally (usually the mother at this age) is withdrawing or withholding her love because of their behaviors that show a growing comfort with separateness, their true self may go into hiding. David Winnicott, a pediatrician-turned-child psychiatrist, draws our attention to how preschool children monitor their parents and will sometimes abandon their authentic self for the sake of retaining the parent's approval, launching a false self based on compliance.[7] When love seems to become conditional at so early an age and the true self is abandoned, the seeds of depression are planted.

Stage 4: Industry (Diligence) vs. Inferiority
Continue Strengthening Trust/Hope/Faith, Autonomy/Willpower, Initiative/Purpose
Components to Add: Industry (Diligence)/Competencies

Erikson used the word *industry* for the next ego strength whose potential arises, linked with the quality of being industrious in acquiring competencies. Using the term industry gives rise to industriousness, which I find awkward, so I often use diligence to refer to the same quality of applying oneself to a goal. As a child matures physically, mentally, and psychologically, they have already been getting their feet wet in the waters of stage 4: developing competencies as they try new tasks. It was evident when they started stacking blocks on the floor at age one and helping dress themselves during their second year. Learning words is a competency. Learning to count. Being industrious and developing competencies doesn't hold off until kindergarten, but mastery of various bodies of knowledge and mental skills valued by one's culture doesn't become a central focus for most children until around age five, and it often continues for the rest of a person's life. Sometimes knowledge and skills come easily and naturally, but often the child must apply themselves diligently. Self-discipline in pursuit of a goal is a valuable tool to acquire, and these years are the ideal time for those who love us to encourage it.

For Erikson, the stage refers in particular to the years of education and skill-building before puberty complicates everything in the social realm and cognitive development ushers in the ability to think abstract thoughts which happens around age twelve. Obviously, it doesn't end with middle school, a fact which makes it clearer that the image of stages is a very loose one indeed. Developing new competencies is a major focus in the high school and college years, and with the beginning of any new job. The abundance or shortage of hope, willpower, and purposefulness (remember: purpose is the free exercise of initiative without having to worry about attachment figures feeling hurt by you living your own life) already in their toolbox greatly affect a child in the larger and more structured environment at school. Without them, they are at a real disadvantage meeting the expectations and measurements of academic progress, as well as the challenges of developing skills in athletics, arts, various organizations, and any trades in which they may begin to train.

At the same time, the new and structured situation of formal schooling provides new opportunities for feedback and interactions that can instill some of the so-called earlier strengths if they have been missing or only faintly developed. As you will see from the stories of my students and clients in part 4, the experience of mattering to a teacher or a coach can be life-changing in far more ways than the simple development of a particular skillset. While teachers and coaches may not treasure us in the same way our family or abiding friends do, they often devote themselves to the well-being of students in ways that convey "You matter to me. This is about more than just a paycheck." Developing competencies in just about any arena helps build confidence that you're capable of learning, capable of becoming competent at other things as well.

You Matter to Me

    Acquiring skills and knowledge as an older child, teenager, and adult can double back and help shore up resources when childhood produced self-doubt, guilt, or feelings of inferiority. An older adult's experience helping a child or teen to develop competencies can be emotionally and psychologically healing for that adult who carries wounds from earlier in life. It's never really over, this chance to heal old wounds, strengthen earlier weaknesses, and pass along strengths to others.

    The kinds of initiative a parent can safely and appropriately endorse and encourage change as a child grows and is ready to exercise increasing independence. Our loved ones continue to thrive when we encourage and support their autonomy, initiative, and competencies throughout life. When we act in ways that help them exercise these metaphorical muscles, we contribute to the deepening of their basic trust and the development of their identity.

Stage 5: Identity vs. Role Confusion
Who Are You?
What Do You Want to Do With These Components, Such As They Are?
What Values are Worth Being Faithful To?
(Continue Developing and Exercising Trust, Autonomy, Initiative, Competencies…)

Hopefully, by now it's really clear that one stage doesn't end just because a new life-task begins to overshadow earlier ones in importance as physical, mental, and even social changes take place. Applying yourself diligently at school, athletic practice, music lessons, or mowing lawns (or in other cultures an older child might already be working at a trade to bring income to the family) continue as hormonal and cognitive changes begin to take place around age eleven or twelve. For some children, the physical changes of puberty come earlier or later than their peers, but when they do come, priorities begin to change as hormones hijack the brain and the rest of the body. And when they come earlier or later than the average, that fact, too, preoccupies the thoughts and self-image of the child becoming a teenager.

Erikson calls adolescence Stage 5: Identity vs. Role Confusion. There's a restless need to sort out what kind of person you want to be and what you want to do with your life and that becomes what matters the most, along with an urgency to belong to a group of some sort whether large or small. As much as anything, there's a need to assert your separateness from your parents, to establish your right to live your own life and make your own decisions. "I'm my own person" is the recurring theme of the adolescent years (an echo of "I want to do it myself!" from toddlerhood). For some, urgency to be in a romantic relationship dominates everything else.

As I've mentioned, I find Erikson's language misleading at this point since identity (and fidelity or loyalty to that identity) isn't another ingredient or resource so much as it is an outcome of a discernment process. This stage, therefore, is a pivot point in his overall schema. What came before are components. He sometimes used the term *virtues* instead of *ego strengths* and particularly for this and the next two stages, I find that word more fitting. The strengths after stage five—mutuality and care—are virtuous/admirable/life-giving ways of being in relationship more than they are characteristics of an individual or components of selfhood. And those virtuous ways of being are more possible and more likely when the already-considered ego strengths characterize a person's self-identity. Because this is true, couples struggling with intimacy/mutuality or with caring for each other and their children well don't need to learn how to communicate with each other better so much as they need to do remedial work on developing the ego strengths so they will feel safe enough to know and be known. Supporting each other in this remedial work is an important part of building trust in the relationship.

Adolescents continue building on earlier skills, exploring new interests, trying out relationships with new kinds of people, and all the while enduring a sense of being on shifting sand.

- What do I enjoy doing?
- What am I good at so far?
- What kind of people do I like being around?
- What do I find satisfying?
- What do I find fulfilling?
- What do I believe gives life meaning?
- What mix of activities allows me to feel balanced, like I'm thriving? and
- What kind of difference do I want to make in the world?

Starting for real at some point in adolescence, a teenager begins using all the character components, weak or strong as they may be, to try and make something happen in their mind and heart—to bring into focus what matters to them and will help them feel on solid ground. These inner needs begin to drive, even haunt some teens earlier than others, and personal self-knowledge comes into focus on different timetables. Some teens have the freedom to explore for many years while others are forced by circumstances outside their control (or sometimes brought about by their own actions, e.g., pregnancy, criminal record, and grades too poor for college) to make choices at a younger age.

In the simplest scenarios, the nucleus of the self's separate identity has been emerging all along, but for many people, the clues are still utterly vague as they go through high school. Parents and others in the person's life can help all along with attunement (see part 3), good mirroring and loving interactions, but even so, the struggle to sort it out is a challenging journey, longer for some than others.

> Ned had doodled in the margins of his school papers ever since grade school. His parents arranged ten weeks of drawing lessons with a local artist when he was in fifth grade. By high school, he was eager for art classes and hoping he could figure out a way to make a living through his love for drawing.

* * * * *

> Pete loved all kinds of sports and played on a team every season. Training, practices, and competitive events consumed all his time and attention. In his teens, being an athlete seemed to be his identity and it continued in college. Although he knew he wasn't going to be a pro, he hadn't paid much attention to what else in life held interest for him. He had plenty of hope, willpower, initiative, and a lot of physical competencies, but in his twenties, he was at a loss for what he wanted to do with his life.

* * * * *

In her teens, Missy felt she had no clue what interested her. Her confidence in herself was shaky due to a lot of upheaval in her past. Her parents had split up when she was small, and she had been looking for affirmation from males ever since. Being chosen by a guy was more important to her than finding herself. When a teen pregnancy led to marriage, the roles of motherhood began to define her. She didn't pay any more attention to questions of who she was or what she wanted. Those questions seemed irrelevant and pointless to her until they resurfaced in her forties when she faced an empty nest.

* * * * *

Sam grew up in a rough neighborhood where acquiring street smarts was the one competency needed for survival. Self-reflection made a guy vulnerable and he had no use for it. He had developed a tough protective shell by the time he was in middle school. His only aspiration was to go live in another town with his older brother, get a job, and start buying the symbols of the good life advertised on TV.

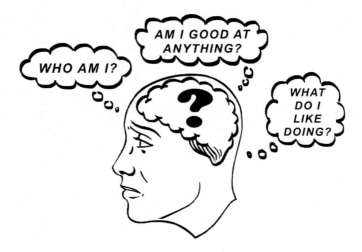

In adolescence, peer feedback becomes far more important than parental input though parents still matter more than most kids want to admit; and teachers, coaches, and bosses can play major roles in the emergence of identity. The need to assert independence—to once again separate from the relationships on which you've been emotionally dependent—becomes among the most important agendas in a teen's life. In the adolescent years, everything's up for grabs as the trust/hope/faith, autonomy/willpower, initiative/purpose, and even some of the competencies that have provided some grounding become relatively devalued. Maybe those components were shaky, maybe they were solid, but those beginnings came from *them* (parents *et al*) and to varying degrees for various teens, that makes them unacceptable, at least for the time being. Some teenagers don't appear to turn away from their parents at all while others are very intentional and public about rejecting what they grew up with.

The years of the identity search are all about hanging out with different people to see if you like what they bring out in you. Figuring out values that matter to you and what you want to spend your time doing while on the planet is the heart of the search for one's self-identity. Erikson says a person needs to crystallize the ego strength of fidelity as part of these years of paying attention to what fulfills you. When you figure out for yourself what really matters to you, you can be faithful/loyal to it—particularly if you have a decent amount of hope, will, purpose, and a sense of being capable of learning and applying yourself to goals you've chosen.

Stage 6: Intimacy vs. Isolation
Are You On a Solo Journey
or In Community With Others
Who Matter To You?
(Continue Developing and Exercising Trust,
Autonomy, Initiative, Competencies…)

Sorting out "who am I?" and "what matters to me in life?" takes different lengths of time for different people. Friendships and dating relationships are inherent parts of this time of searching, experimenting, and trying out new aspects of who you are and who you might want to be. And in the midst of those relationships, a person may begin taking the emotional risks inherent in intimacy—the experience of sharing what's deeper inside than meets the eye. Intimacy's opposite is isolation—the painful experience of not being known and not knowing anyone else well enough to feel genuinely connected. The ego strength Erikson names as the accomplishment of stage 6 is *mutuality*—taking each other's well-being into account as you make choices in life. Mutual love like this is possible only if you know each other at deeper-than-superficial levels. Modifying your own individual agenda for the sake of someone who matters to you may come easily some of the time, but approaching life that way consistently over the long haul is an ongoing challenge and accomplishment.

In contemporary society, intimacy has become synonymous with physical and especially sexual closeness, but it's important to reclaim its broader meaning if you're going to understand what this capacity of the self is really all about. Intimacy is openness. It's taking the risk of opening yourself up and being seen by someone else, hopefully someone worthy of your trust. In their book on marriage, Andrew and Judith Lester identify several areas of any person's life in which two people can share themselves superficially or deeply: intellectually, emotionally, physically (nonsexually as well as sexually), spiritually, and socially (which involves being open about what takes place in their social realms and how those other relationships affect them)[8]. I add the category of "psychologically" since I don't think it's fully covered by the emotional realm. It involves knowledge of the personal history that helps explain what makes a person tick—why a person's thoughts, emotions, wants, and actions interact the way they do.

Intimacy—sharing the intricacies of your genuine true self as best you are able and/or discovering those intricacies in open conversation with someone you trust—is life-giving. Some of my clients over the years have told me that only by trying to tell me who they are have they found out who they are and what matters to them. In other words, they have discovered and formed their true self through the therapy relationship. Ideally, people do that very thing through trustworthy intimate friendships. Sometimes, this depth of sharing happens across the sexual divide and sometimes with members of the same sex. Personal histories with parents and siblings, neighbors, and friends can create biases that steer people toward trusting one sex or the other. At its core, intimacy is not sexual but spiritual in that it is sharing at the level of true selves, the level where souls connect. Although it can broaden to include sexual intimacy if both people consent, it does not have to in order to be richly fulfilling of the soul's need for emotional, psychological, and spiritual intimacy. In some instances, the move to sexual intimacy complicates the relationship so much that soul intimacy actually gets lost.

Intimacy and trust are intertwined, of course. Some of our deepest wounds come from having misplaced our trust and shared vulnerable aspects of ourselves with people who abused the faith we placed in them. Doubling back and establishing the ability to trust in adulthood when mistrust was sewn in childhood or adolescence is not an easy job, though it can be done if the person with whom you risk intimacy is capable of loving well. It is generally a slow process akin to the taming described in the classic tale *The Little Prince,* truly a labor of love requiring patience and devotion.[9]

Intimacy and mutual love are the ultimate accomplishment in interpersonal human relationships. It is possible between friends, spouses, siblings, even parents and children who have matured in their relationship beyond the power struggles inherent in growing up. It is a product of trust/hope/faith, even if it's only fledgling trust in someone still rehabilitating from childhood's deficiencies. And when it is honored and protected as a sacred trust by both persons, it deepens basic trust/hope/faith into a source of resilience at the core of a solid marriage. It can't be dependent on the feelings/emotion dimension of love. It takes attitude. Above all, it takes a desire to be that kind of self-giving person whether you feel like it at the moment or not. Loving another person deeply can make you want to become the kind of person who will love them well, not just now, but always. Becoming that kind of person is a long-term life goal.

Stage 7: Generativity vs. Stagnation
Using Your Self to Create and Care For the Next Generation and/or the World Around You
(Continue Developing and Exercising Trust, Autonomy, Initiative, Competencies, Consolidating a Sense of Self and Practicing Mutual Love...)

Usually, the long process of sorting out one's identity intermingles with trying out intimacy in various relationships. Sometimes people make babies together, with or without benefit of marriage, before finding out whether or not their not-yet-crystallized identities and their goals in life are compatible. I've had many clients through the years struggling with marriages that were coming apart because that was how they had started; neither has ever been completely certain the other would have chosen them if there hadn't been a baby on the way. I've had other clients who were the children of marriages that started that way; some of them carry a core belief that "I am the problem." Thankfully, many marriages that begin this way are between two people who bring inner resources, facilitate each other's growth, and learn how to love each other well.

Caregiving can become a problematic part of a person's accommodating false self early in life if that's the only way to receive acceptance and affirmation in the family. Unfortunately, if caregiving becomes a person's primary way of connecting, their relationships may be more about their own need to be needed than about the recipient's actual needs.[10] The ability to attune to the other person's competencies as well as their needs is part of the larger skill I will discuss in part 3. Significantly, the freedom to attune can be greatly hampered by preoccupation with one's own mistrust, self-doubt, guilt, and feelings of inadequacy, all undercurrents created by unmet needs that pull and distort a person's awareness, making it hard to tune in to a loved one.

Erikson's generativity concept includes whatever you spend your adult energy, time, and talents on. For many, though not all by any means, those years are dominated by raising children and, hopefully, loving them well enough to help them launch effectively into their own adulthoods. Employment and career are also arenas of being productive, creative, and demonstrating care.

What's important for you to understand is this: the capacity to care identified by Erikson is all about loving other people into having the ego strengths we've been talking about, whatever their age or relationship to you. It's about loving them into wholeness and health. So when you read examples of sustaining, supporting, or confronting in part 4, I hope it will come alive for you that people are typically reengaging several of the various ego strengths (or weaknesses) at any given time your life intersects with theirs. One person working on becoming competent at something in their adult workplace (and maybe struggling against their feelings of inferiority) may be simultaneously engaged in caring for their child by coaching the soccer team; they may also be benefiting from the way their spouse is affirming their desire to develop some friendships around kayaking (overcoming the twinges of guilt that come up because of messages from their parents during their teenage years about spending too much time with friends). We are complex beings and we need all the genuine love we can get, which oddly enough includes the opportunity to give it to others.

In summary, all of us are reworking the various teeter-totters Erikson identified (x vs. y) all the time. Do I trust or mistrust this person? Do I feel autonomous in this situation or full of self-doubt? Do I feel okay about taking initiative or worried about whether the relationship can handle it? No, we don't actually formulate the tensions in these very words, but these are the internal issues working themselves out within our relationships. All of us are working on the challenges of everyday life and relationships at whatever our age. If we've incorporated healthy amounts of trust, autonomy, initiative, and diligence (of hope, will, purpose, and competence) into our sense of "This is who I am," we will probably be capable of forming a mature adult relationship of mutuality and capable of caring for the next generation and the community around us. And we will probably have enough resilience to handle most of what life brings our way—with a little help from our friends!

Stage 8: Integrity vs. Despair
The Retirement Years—Continuing to Care and Looking Back (Hopefully) with a Sense of Wisdom on a Life That's Had Integrity (Continue Developing and Exercising Trust, Autonomy, Initiative, Competencies, Consolidating a Sense of Self, Practicing Mutual Love and Care…)

Although Erikson was working on a postretirement stage at the time of his death, the last of his fully articulated stages is called Integrity vs. Despair. It is an acknowledgement that at some point in the later years, whenever a person begins to see their most productive years as behind them, they tend to review their life on a number of measures. In Erikson's view, those who have had the benefit of enough of the ego strengths are more likely to experience the satisfaction of a life well lived, having had fulfilling relationships and made meaningful contributions to the world around them. They sense that although there may have been regrettable lapses, by and large their lives have had integrity—that is to say it has been their true self who has lived life, true to the values they came to recognize as most important to them. Along the way, they have learned what makes life worth living and are therefore regarded as having wisdom. Erikson speaks of a wisdom that comes from making peace with yourself as life winds down. It's a peace and wisdom I saw in my father in his eighties, a man who had fought in a war, married his true love and raised three children, worked in state government to help people find jobs, served on boards to improve his community, cared for aging parents and relatives, and buried his wife of fifty-seven years and missed her daily, but found enjoyment in life in the retirement community to which they had moved together. When he died at ninety-two, he was a man who had been true to his values and had loved well.

Even if a stage addressing the retirement years is conceptualized and put forth by the heirs of Erikson's work, integrity vs. despair must remain the chronologically last one in the series. The notion that the postretirement years should be more self-indulgent rather than work-oriented is more a product of the Social Security Act than an observation about human nature in general. Generativity and care continue to be the defining categories for most of adulthood, regardless of a societal designation of sixty-five or seventy as the appropriate age to retire from the paid workforce. Perhaps it would be enough to simply recognize that our ways of being productive and the targets of our care evolve throughout our adult years. Thus, rather than trying to envision a new, additional stage with its own particular crisis, Erikson's original schema can stay in place with a much longer and more varied stage 7.

Ideally, the seeds of the ego strengths are planted in us in childhood, grow stronger in adolescence, become part of the personal identity we bring into adulthood and continue crystallizing within intimate friendships and intimate marriage. Ideally, having been loved well, we become cascades that spill over to love others well. And ideally, because few life stories are really ideal, we see the places our loved ones struggle and we try to love them in ways that repair, build up, restore, and heal what may not have gone so well in their pasts. We try to become a source of hope because our love is trustworthy, a supporter of will and initiative, someone who helps them acquire competencies, a safe conversation partner for sorting out questions of "who am I really?" a listener worthy of being entrusted with still tender self-revelations. Loving one another into greater wholeness and greater resilience is a way of life.

Yes, things go wrong even for those who are well-equipped and have the best intentions…

What I have laid out is the ideal and it rarely (probably never!) happens that a child is the recipient of all the life circumstances and interpersonal feedback that makes for the optimal development of the optimally resilient character structure. Life happens. I just read on Facebook the shortened obituary of the mother of a German acquaintance. The mother had been a child affected by WWI in her early years while her core internal resources were taking shape. By the time WWII came along, she had become a young adult trying to develop a marriage and care for children. The world around her drastically affected how (first) her parents and then how she, herself, could carry out the actions that devoted love wants very much to provide. Wars happen.

Illnesses happen, taking away or co-opting the availability and attention of caregivers. For instance, any three-year-old's life inevitably changes when a second baby is born, but Tom was affected more than most when his sister was born with lung trouble. Emergency surgery was followed by the family's relocation to a city with a hospital specializing in children's health. Ongoing respiratory scares and periodic surgeries dominated the family's life from that point forward. His parents did the best they could for the healthy older child as he continued to grow even while they responded to their baby's needs. He developed some ego strengths more fully than he might have otherwise—and some less.

Accidents and deaths happen. As a child, Mary was in a car accident in which her younger brother was killed. Her mother had been driving, and never got over it. Her mother's complicated grief, oppressive guilt feelings, and fear for Mary's safety dominated the atmosphere in their home and limited the freedom Mary had for exercising autonomy and developing competencies and her identity.

Children are born with physical problems and limitations that create their own challenges. Sara was born with a congenital heart defect that necessitated surgeries throughout her childhood. Day to day life revolved around her medical care and that shaped her own development of the ego strengths, as well as her older brother's.

Children are born with temperaments that make it easy or just downright challenging for parents to foster the development of ego strengths. Nick was a quiet baby who was easy to care for. He received plenty of cherishing from his parents, and they encouraged his explorations and interests in every way they could. In contrast, Teddy was high-strung from the time he was born, tested all the limits constantly as he grew, and necessitated more "no's" than the average child.

And then there are the parents themselves, individuals who come to parenthood shaped by their own developmental histories. Bill's mother had been wounded, herself, at an early age by her own mother's choice to leave her husband and children. Her basic trust had been shaken by this experience of maternal rejection, and self-doubt was the undercurrent of her life as a result. Understandably, her ways of providing care to her children were shaped as much or more by her own need for reassurance and affirmation (compensating for her mistrust, self-doubt, and inferiority) as by what Bill and his siblings actually needed and were ready for as they grew.

And even the best parental efforts by the psychologically healthiest adults are being interpreted by…children! And children have an extremely limited frame of reference and simplistic abilities to make sense of what's happening around them. Molly's father lost his job due to the economic slump and was unemployed for a year and a half. At age seven, she knew he used to go away to work every day and now he didn't, but she believed her mother's edginess and her father's irritability were because of *her*. So she overused her autonomy to take care of her siblings and herself, be largely invisible, and make few demands on them. She limited her exercise of initiative and pursuit of any purposes that might take her off on her own since she felt very insecure about what was happening at home.

Even with all these caveats, by identifying the components of a resilient self, Erikson brought into focus the goals of loving well. The loved one may be a child whose physical and mental (cognitive) growth are making it possible to develop one of the building blocks for the very first time at the age Erikson identified as chronologically appropriate. Or they may be a grown-up spouse, colleague, or friend who reacts to situations and circumstances in ways that make no sense to you—because of the unfinished business of components insufficiently developed in childhood and adolescence. Though all of us bring what Gottman calls *enduring vulnerabilities* with us into adulthood, i.e. sensitivities to certain negative events, Erikson's framework provides a lens for understanding the strengths and weaknesses in ourselves and others. Such understanding can help us love one another more effectively, especially when we employ the skills of attunement described in part 3.

Part 3: Love Pays Attention

5

Attunement—the Way to Build and Maintain Trust

John Gottman's long-term research with couples has provided proof in the marital realm of what we're known in the therapy realm for a long time: empathic attunement is what establishes trust. What is empathic attunement? It's paying enough attention to another person to pick up what they communicate through their body language, facial expressions, and tone of voice along with what they verbalize in words. You may not have thought much about it consciously, but when you are interacting with someone in person, you are processing far more information than simply their words. Research has shown that if the nonverbal and verbal messages don't match up, in all likelihood you'll believe your interpretation of the nonverbals[1]. So, for instance, if a parent or spouse says "I'm not angry at you," but the tension in their voice, the muscles in their forehead, or the way they're holding their body convey anger, you simply will not believe those words. No wonder comedians so easily get a laugh by having one person say "There's nothing wrong" when every nonverbal is screaming "I'm upset with you!"

Paul Ekman's international research has argued persuasively that there are universal human emotions that show up in the same way on the human face, regardless of the culture in which the person is raised. For instance, there is no culture where the lip pulled slightly sideways matches up with the emotion of sorrow or a furrowed brow matches up with joy. No, a sneer (what Ekman calls the *dimpler* look because pulling the mouth sideways creates a dimple) conveys contempt wherever you are in the world and whenever you find yourself in human history and joy is readable in a smile and a light in someone's eyes.[2] Screenwriters and movie directors count on the near-universality of these facts. Although some people make a priority out of learning to suppress the facial muscles, it's hard to mask them completely and facial signs of the basic emotions of joy, sorrow, contempt, disgust, anger, and surprise are usually evident to anyone paying attention. Individuals whose lives depend on accurately detecting deceit in another person can be trained to read even the tiniest muscle clues in the face and especially around the eyes of other people. Paying attention is the important point here. When it matters enough, we can learn how to pay attention.

Children begin to gather information from nonverbal messages long before words take on any meaning to them. As childhood progresses into adolescence, different people become more and less motivated to develop and use the skill of tuning in to other people. As I've already noted, some children develop finely tuned radars to pick up the moods of key people in their homes, and they tend to keep relying on their antennae throughout life, typically quite certain they are reading other people accurately. This is particularly true in homes where one person's moods had a huge and predictable impact on the child's well-being. Other children seem to leave their ability underdeveloped, sometimes because their parents don't teach them the skills and at other times because of a self-centeredness that leaves them unmotivated to pay attention to the feelings and nonverbal messages of other people. Still others essentially shut down their emotion radars because what they pick up is far too overwhelming. For most of us, childhood yields an average motivation and ability to read the emotional cues of others, with females showing a somewhat higher natural inclination and ability than males on average.[3]

Gottman focused his observational research on children and their parents early in his career. He studied the parenting styles in eighty-six families with children aged four and five, gathering vast amounts of information through questionnaires and interviews. He had his research students observe parent-child interactions closely, looking for signs of empathy and parental attunement to the child. Perhaps most importantly, he used scientific methods to measure what was actually taking place in the child's autonomic (involuntary) nervous system[4] while they were interacting with their parents around intense issues. He discovered that when parents put their devotion into action by using five simple skills when the child's anger, fear, or sadness are intense, those children generally turn out to be emotionally healthy and likely to become effective parents themselves. He and his colleagues call the following skills *emotion coaching*:

1. Notice the negative emotion before it escalates.
2. Seeing it as an opportunity for teaching or intimacy.
3. Validating or empathizing with the emotion.
4. Helping the child give verbal labels to all emotions the child is feeling.
5. Setting limits on misbehavior, or problem-solving if there is no misbehavior. If the parent doesn't do whit last step, the kids tend to wind up becoming physically or verbally aggressive toward other children.[5]

Following the children over time, the researchers saw evidence that children parented by good emotion coaches developed an awareness and tolerance of their own inner experiences and a readiness to empathize with others—a capacity Gottman calls emotional intelligence. Children parented in these ways made better grades, were in better physical health, had fewer reports of behavioral problems or violent behaviors, and were regarded by teachers as more socially competent with their peers.

Gottman argues persuasively that a child who experiences safe connection with parents during emotional upheavals in childhood is more likely to develop the capacity for emotional self-regulation. We know this capacity is important for learning and relationship because many research neuropsychiatrists, most notably Stephen Porges, have shown that when a person's emotions are highly charged, their whole nervous system is hijacked by primitive fight, flight, or freeze reactions that severely limit the brain's ability to learn and to connect socially.[6] Gottman argues convincingly that safe connectedness even when upset is what allows a child to remain in an integrative learning state of body and mind. When parents are able to regulate their own strong emotions while coaching their young child through intense situations, children develop better impulse control and the ability to soothe themselves when upset. They also learn to read the emotional cues of others, delay gratification, focus their attention, and cope better with life's ups and downs. These skills help account for their greater success on so many measures.

As time passed, Gottman's research interests turned to adult relationships and he set up an apartment lab where he and his assistants could record and study the minutia of couples interacting. In their close observation of couples, Gottman's team discovered that the same attunement skills that contribute to children trusting their parents' love also contribute to whether spouses trust each other's love. In other words, men and women are gauging whether they matter to each other in much the same way children are gauging whether they matter to and can be themselves with their parents.

Gottman noticed couples giving many subtle and not-so-subtle indications they'd like the other person's attention or response, and he called these *bids*. He designated the different responses the partner might make as turning toward, turning away, or turning against. (See next section.) He discovered that whether partners turn towards, away, or against each other especially when something negative is going on for one or both of them is a very significant predictor of the relationship surviving.[7] Gottman's work brings into focus that bids and turning, in general, are extremely important in establishing basic trust in childhood and in every relationship thereafter. It's also clear that responses to bids move the needle on the Matter Meter and they add supplies to the water tank or punch holes in it.

As he learned in his work with parents and children, attunement is a skillset most easily learned by a child whose parents model it for them early in life. Nevertheless, the skills can be learned by just about anyone who really wants to learn how to empathize with other people.

Gottman captured the skills in an acronym[8]:

ATTUNE

Awareness of the emotion
Turning toward the emotion
Tolerance of the emotional experience
Understanding the emotion
Non-defensive listening to the emotion
Empathy toward the emotion

(If you're a stickler for accuracy, you'll notice that the fourth and fifth words are not in the right logical order -- that is, you have to listen before you can understand and empathize. Gottman has rearranged them for the acronym to work.)

It's worth noting that you have to value another person before empathizing with them will seem important to you. Bids and turning permeate relationships of every kind, but our concern here is attuning purely for the sake of loving another person well. (Some people make a priority of attuning to others as a way to use those people. For instance, they want to figure out how to influence them or to market to them, so they have an ulterior motive to figuring out what makes them tick.) Let's look more closely now at these individual elements of attunement.

(Be) Aware

Poring over thousands of minutes of couple interactions, Gottman and his colleagues recognized that people are continually signaling they want some kind of connection with the other person and he calls those various verbal and nonverbal signals bids. Being aware means paying enough attention to at least pick up those signals. The desire may be for minimal acknowledgement such as a raised eyebrow to neutrally signal "I see you've come into the room" or for a smile that signals "I'm glad you've come." Or the bid may be for a more major connection such as conversation, a request that you do something like bring a glass of water when you come back from the kitchen, or for humor or affection.

In the Science of Trust, Gottman gives these examples of ways of making bids for some kind of recognition or connection:

1. A bid for attention
2. Simple requests (e.g. "While you're up, get me the butter.")
3. A bid for help, teamwork, or coordination (e.g. help with an errand)
4. A bid for the partner's interest or active excitement
5. Questions or requests for information
6. A bid for conversation
7. A bid for just venting
8. Sharing events of the day
9. Stress reduction
10. Problem solving
11. Humor, laughter

12. Affection
13. Playfulness
14. Adventure
15. Exploration
16. Learning something together
17. Intimate conversation
18. Emotional support
19. Understanding, compassion, empathy
20. Sexual intimacy

Bids often come in the form of facial expressions, body language, or tone of voice. Others are expressed in words, sometimes clearly and at other times ambiguously. People who know each other well often develop a silent language of bids and responses to bids without even consciously thinking about it.

Ways of Making Bids

Bids come in the form of facial expressions like a smile or frown, body language like sitting with your head down in your hands, outright verbal requests or comments, and actions such as offering your hand to shake or rolling your neck in hopes of getting a shoulder massage.

- Facial expressions—frown, smile, furrowed brow, scowl, pout, curious, sad, and discouraged;
- Body language—slumped posture, rolling a stiff neck to stretch it, bounciness, and crossed arms (if not relaxing);
- Verbal—clear throat, ask a question, ask for help, laugh, make an idle comment about something, tell about an event, and make a direct request; and
- Actions—slam a door, peek into a room, flirt, touch gently, kiss, and start doing a task.

Carol J. Sherman, PhD

Turn Toward

It doesn't take a research scientist to tell us we all use nonverbals day in and day out to communicate with each other, but the meticulous observational work done by Gottman's assistants established that it's the way people *responded to* the bids that had a major and predictable impact. It became clear that the patterns of responses over time affect trust levels in the relationship. Positive responses that ranged anywhere from minimal acknowledgment to enthusiastic engagement were labeled *turning toward*. If the person responded in a grumpy, irritated, annoyed, or aggressive manner, it was labeled *turning against*. And if the person didn't respond at all—as if they hadn't heard or noticed the bid at all even though it was likely it had registered on their senses—it was labeled *turning away*. This last one, of course, assumes the person did register the bid with one or more of the five senses and sometimes that's not the case. Sometimes the bidder believes they've been ignored when what actually happened was the person's hearing is faulty or they actually didn't see the bid. Unfortunately, if a relationship is in the process of eroding, people tend to assume the worst—that they are being intentionally ignored. We send off e-mail and text bids many times a day, assuming they arrive at the intended destination and when we get no response, we often interpret this as being turned away from or turned against. The fact that many of our electronic bids are delayed, routed into junk mail, or lost entirely in cyberspace results in many unfortunate wounds and fights that would not happen if the two people had a regular and reliable habit of replying with "got it."

Turning toward builds the good will in the relationship—what some call the emotional bank account—such that when there is a conflict, it's more likely the two will work it through positively. Turning away and particularly turning against erode good will and add to a general mood of negativity and sense of pessimism. Building on the work of Robert Weis, Gottman calls this situation negative sentiment override, a relationship condition in which the pessimism has gotten so strong that even when the partner does do something positive, it doesn't count. In this kind of environment, conflict is more likely since people are primed to take offense. And when injuries do happen, efforts to make things right again are less likely to be effective.

If you're overflowing with tenderness toward a baby you're holding—or a child or a spouse—and that loved one doesn't want to be held at that moment, they are not experiencing "I'm treasured" but "I'm intruded upon" or "I'm suffocating." Just as attunement in general builds trust, recognizing misattunement quickly is important so that you can make repairs, which also builds trust. As you'll see in my explanation of treasuring in part 4, attuning is the initial step which allows us to accurately match the subsequent actions of love to the actual condition of our loved one. The match communicates to the loved one "You really do know me and you care enough to provide what I need, not just what you feel like giving."

Even when good will is prevailing, we are all guilty of sometimes being careless, inconsiderate, inept, selfish, etc. Therefore regrettable incidents happen in all relationships, even the most loving ones. What matters, says Gottman, is how quickly we attempt to repair the misstep and how open the injured party is to accepting the repair, both of which are greatly affected by whether there is good will in the bank. He calls repairs the secret medicine of couples who have strong relationships. On the way to the sixtieth wedding anniversary celebration for a couple we both knew, a friend asked the husband the secret to their long marriage. His answer? "A readiness to forgive." I have no doubt Gottman would count this couple among the masters of relationship.

It's not necessary to get it right every time, but evidence of the desire to notice and turn toward bids will build trust even when you get the details of the response wrong some of the time. When this effort is missing over and over again, the Matter Meter chronically measures low.

Tolerate

The notion of tolerating in the attunement paradigm is especially important when what the loved one is expressing is something negative such as anger, frustration, fear, anxiety, jealousy, sadness, etc. Much of the time, we'd prefer not to stop what we're doing and engage the unpleasantness. That's especially true if we know or suspect we are contributors to their reaction or mood, but even if it's not about us, we're often reluctant to provide the time and energy to engage. Even if we do stop, we're often more interested in talking them out of their feelings than tolerating those feelings long enough to connect with the person in a meaningful way.

As I explained in chapter 3, love relationships often begin with an illusory period of believing "we're the same" or "we're so much alike it'll always be easy to work things out." As the evidence emerges over time that we often want and need different things than our loved one, so does the autonomy-protecting assertion of the will so evident in early childhood and adolescence. The more unfinished business an adult has from those early experiences of having their freedom curtailed by parents, the more likely it is that power struggles will quickly arise in adult relationships. People often make bids in negative ways, using what the authors of *Connecting with Self and Others* would call Fight Talk or Spite Talk. (See Appendix C.) It's very hard *not* to turn against such bids, responding in those same hurtful styles. Exercising self-discipline over the attitudes and feelings that get triggered—the reactions of an inner child or teenage part of your personality with unfinished business—is a crucial feature of devotion to the relationship. Developing a habit of tolerance when a loved one is upset about something is the outward evidence of that self-discipline, a habit that makes room for the next steps of attuning.

Nondefensively Listen

The Gottmans put understanding next to make the acronym work, but I'm going to explain the nondefensive listening in its appropriate place in the order. Reining in your impulse to assert your own agenda is hard work. The goal is to make space to listen with a true desire to receive the other person's experience of the situation. It's hard work to contain the two-year-old and/or fourteen-year-old inside you that are chomping at the bit to assert "but what about me?!?" More often than not, the inner chatter of those younger versions of yourself instantly comes up with defenses and counterarguments to everything your loved one is saying. It's so very hard to truly stay focused on receiving information about the other person's experience. And if they're saying you are part of the problem, it's often hard to accept a portion of responsibility for what's gone wrong. (Being willing to do so instead of being defensive is one of the "antidotes" the Gottmans identify for couples trying to get back on track and rebuild trust.) In a relationship practicing mutuality, the commitment by both persons to grant this kind of open listening to the other person builds trust.[9] This skill is of particular importance in implementing the Challenge Love I call confronting respectfully. In Appendix D, you'll find a list of techniques to help you calm yourself down so you can listen better.

Understand

The word *understand* has many synonyms that imply quite a range of meanings, all the way from thoroughly realizing and fathoming something from the inside out to simply being aware of and sympathizing. In the context of how attunement builds and maintains trust, trying to understand the other person means nondefensively listening for the sake of learning everything you can about your loved one's experience and history that's relevant to the issue at hand. Your goal is to make sense of how the thoughts, feelings, and past actions about whatever issue the data has triggered help explain your loved one's recent or present actions, their wants, and the future actions they're considering. In contrast to body language that conveys "hurry up and finish so I can talk," effective, active listening invites more than just the minimal sharing. Active listening seeks further information by asking open questions: who, where, what, when, and how (*not why* which automatically triggers defensiveness).[10]

Empathy

Empathy is the capacity to get inside another person's head and body (figuratively, of course, based on the information they provide) and experience whatever the issue may be as if you were that person. Of course, no one can do this fully, but it starts with recognizing that "If I'd had the same life experiences as you've had, I might very well be responding as you're responding." The humility of that recognition motivates the next steps: "Help me know the data you're responding to and what you're thinking and feeling about it." That will help you better understand what's leading them to want whatever it is they want.

As I said above, the capacity for empathizing is more developed in some people than others, and there are brain-based sex differences as to how male and female brains perceive and process emotional data. What matters most in love relationships, however, is whether you're motivated to try. Even if a person is very clumsy at reading a loved one's emotional cues, their desire to do so counts for a lot in the eyes of the loved one.

Gottmann's observational research and his insights into attunement as the foundation of trust are helpful underpinnings to developmental theories like Erikson's and Mahler's. If you want your loved one to believe they matter to you, there's no better place to begin than by learning the skills of attunement.

Part 4:
Love in Action—Love Treasures

Treasuring

Nurture Love	Challenge Love
Cherish	Support
Sustain	Teach/Coach
	Pollinate with Insights
	Confront Differences Respectfully
	Take a Firm Stand

We've looked together at the attributes love seeks to build up in the loved one, whatever their age. We've looked at the kind of attentiveness it takes to tune in and discover what's going on right here and now with this loved one so that you have a chance at being well-guided in how to most effectively show your love for them. No, you won't always get it right, but when a person really knows your efforts arise from treasuring them, they will usually forgive your mistakes.

It's time now to look closely at the third strand of that strong rope that makes up love at its best: actions. There are particular kinds of actions that help bring about a loved one's well-being, that help create trust/hope, autonomy/willpower, initiative/purpose, industry (diligence)/competence, and foster the development of a true self-identity to which a person wants to be faithful/loyal and devoted so that self-respect is a natural outcome. I have identified certain types of actions that nurture a loved one just as they are and other types of actions that participate with them as life challenges them to grow, develop, and fulfill their potential as a uniquely gifted person.

Before I discuss each of these categories of action separately, I want to talk about the all-encompassing concept of treasuring another person, of experiencing that person as somehow a part of you, as having a place in your heart. This is very different from valuing someone because you've decided via reasoning that they ought to be important to you (i.e., they are your duty, or because taking care of them well makes them more useful to you in some way).

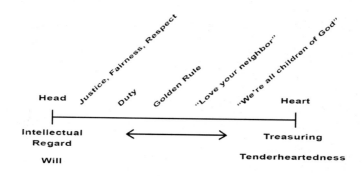

As you can see in the gradient above, sometimes acts that promote another person's well-being are motivated by philosophical reasons and implemented by acts of the will. Those very same acts can also be motivated by tenderheartedness that arises when you experience another person as somehow essential to your own sense of self, as "in your heart." Many weddings include Saint Paul's description of love as found in the Christian Bible:

> Love is patient, love is kind. It does not envy, it does not boast, it is not proud. It does not dishonor others, it is not self-seeking, it is not easily angered, it keeps no record of wrongs. Loves does not delight in evil but rejoices with the truth. It always protects, always trusts, always, hopes, always perseveres. Love never fails.
>
> 1 Corinthians 13: 4-8, New International Version

Anyone who has tried to live up to this ideal discovers that tenderheartedness alone cannot be relied on to carry it out.

Our love for someone we treasure is unconditional. Yes, they probably do meet some of our needs, but that's not why we love them. They do nothing to earn it, and there seems to be an infinite amount of it. Even when patience and self-control grow thin and run out, the desire for that treasured person's well-being doesn't end.

YOU ARE WHAT FILLS MY TREASURE CHEST!

This message is particularly important to give during a child's terrible twos and again in their tumultuous teens. In both of those life stages, it's difficult for parents to find the balance between supporting the autonomy of their blossoming child or teen and protecting them from the possibly negative consequences of those explorations. Handling the push-pull of a teen's normal separation phase can turn parents prematurely gray. Dana captured the picture well as she described her teen years and how her mom handled the challenge:

Carol J. Sherman, PhD

As a teenager, I was like every other girl my age: awkward. I was trying to find myself, develop self-esteem, and fit in. In order to find the self I could be true to, I needed to try on different identities. Most teenagers use their friends for feedback, but for me it was my mom. I tried a million religions, dyed my light blonde hair maroon, wore all black, pierced my own nose, and started dating a guy four years older than myself. Despite all of these rebellious behaviors that I'm sure frustrated my parents no end and which led to my father refusing to let me out of the house half the time, my mother was my biggest supporter through it all. No matter what, she accepted me and encouraged me to express myself in whatever ways I felt comfortable. She understood that if wearing all black and dying my hair made me feel more like myself, then that was what I needed to do. I'm sure she wasn't a 150 percent thrilled with some of my choices back then, but she was 250 percent supportive of *me*. She loved me because I was me. Despite my purple hair and obnoxious nose ring, she loved me. One morning in particular sticks out in memory, a day I still reflect on eight years later. I was probably fifteen or sixteen and very uncomfortable with my body and appearance. I was running late for school, as usual, but I could never leave without saying "good-bye" to my mom. I was in a bad mood, hating the way I looked, but I didn't have time to change or find something I felt more comfortable wearing. I rushed into my mother's room to say "good-bye," and she looked at me and told me that I looked beautiful. My response to her was a very nasty "No I don't" before I rushed out the door, but that moment stuck in my mind. It wasn't until a long time after that I realized my mother was very much aware of what I was going through that morning and was more than willing to offer up whatever help she could to meet my needs.

People often choose to make a positive difference in the lives of others just because they're a fellow human being or we're all part of the human family. Any time we provide sustaining, supporting, coaching/teaching, pollinating, respectful confronting, or firm boundary setting by taking a stand with someone who matters to us in their own right (rather than as a means to a personal end of our own) it's a manifestation of love whether there is tenderheartedness or not. Many of the actions I'll be describing as love can be done out of care or affection rather than treasuring. When a sense of kinship with someone who is hurting or in need moves us to carry out love's actions even to complete strangers, we call that manifestation of love compassion.

With a broader understanding that love is acting with another's well-being at heart even if we don't tenderly treasure that person, my students often begin to recognize they have been loved by teachers, coaches, or neighbors and that they, themselves, have loved complete strangers. The Greeks had several different words for love having to do with the nature of the relationship between the two people: *philia* for friendship, *storge* for parental and sibling types of family relationships, *eros* for romantic relationships (In his book *The Four Loves*, C. S. Lewis adds *venus* to differentiate sexual lust from romance), and *agape* for unconditional love. But even these don't sufficiently get at the distinction I'm making because even within these groupings, there are some individuals in each category whom we experience as part of our very selves and others we don't. Sometimes we feel tenderhearted toward the people we do treasure and sometimes we don't. These are realities many of us experience, but few of us bother sorting them out clearly enough to really understand what conveys the reality of treasuring or what's missing when it's absent or has disappeared.

The Nurture Loves

As you read about the various actions that keep a person alive and healthy or facilitate their growth in various ways, it's important to realize that the recipient of your actions cannot know your motive for any action unless you reveal it to them. You could be acting in ways that look like Nurture Love and Challenge Love primarily out of duty or self-interest instead of heartfelt treasuring of the other person. Most of us know that there's a noticeable difference in what it feels like for someone to be there for us out of duty instead of because they really want to be present and/or involved. Yes, there are people who are great actors and if faking it matters to them enough, they can fool someone who is really naïve. But most people aren't that motivated to pretend or they can't pull it off very well. A child can sense from a very young age if a caregiver's heart isn't in it, and it makes a difference for that child's love tank, their belief that they matter.

I use the term *cherish* for the particular actions that clearly and unmistakably communicate this larger reality that *"You have a place in my heart. All these other things I do to facilitate your well-being are coming from this inner reality."* Many a recipient of the other six love actions longs to believe they are enacted out of treasuring, but if certain particular cherishing behaviors are missing—behaviors I will specify below—they doubt whether it's really true. When this "I treasure you" message has been clearly given via cherishing actions and has been received, basic trust and hope are securely planted in the person's core and continue to grow.

If this message is effectively given to a child from the start, their heart remains open to others, unguarded by the need for overly protective walls.[1] When I speak of a person's heart, I am speaking of that person's innermost true self, the kernel of "I-ness," the core experience of subjectivity that, if all goes well enough, will become the center of that person's emerging identity in adolescence and young adulthood. The seed of true self in a newborn is unguarded and yearning to connect. If that seed lands in the fertile soil of parents who welcome that child into their own hearts and who are able to create a stable-enough environment, the true self of the child begins to thrive and grow stronger. If the parents communicate their treasuring well, and if they carry out the other actions I will describe well enough, the child's true self grows and begins accumulating the ego strengths Erikson identified. In this optimal situation, the heart/true self doesn't feel vulnerable and need to live behind excessively self-protective barriers as life unfolds.

If, on the other hand, one or more of the primary caregivers is a cause of pain or prolonged loneliness (due to abuse and/or neglect) or if illness, injuries, or absences link the caregiver with pain or sadness in the child's mind through the process of classical conditioning, the child will add more and more protective layers around their heart.[2] I picture this process as creating what I call *Plexiglas* around the heart. If Plexiglas starts surrounding the heart early in life, the true self remains guarded behind this protective wall. Others can see the image that person shows the world, but can't experience who they really are inside or feel connected with them in deeper than superficial ways. They'll only let you know them, get inside them, up to a certain point and then it's as if you run into a wall. In some cases when Plexiglas is needed for safety, the child will be significantly hampered in their quest to develop autonomy and willpower, to exercise initiative and pursue their unique interests, to develop competencies and grow toward an identity directly linked to the authentic true self. In other cases, the child will develop a fierce need for autonomy and will separate prematurely, a stance in life I call *counterdependence* to distinguish it from healthy independence on the way to interdependence. Counterdependence is a survival tactic to avoid being dependent when earlier relationships had proven disappointing or dangerous. When Plexiglas forms early, the child unconsciously creates a false, accommodating self, as described by Winnicott, to interact with others and get on with life. Forever after, these children/teens/adults continually guard against establishing true intimacy for fear of someone discovering that behind the public mask is a vulnerable true self despairing of a chance at resilience. People can get very good at living multiple lives, accommodating to more than one person's expectations of them while still hiding the core true self. Needless to say, living this way uses up a lot of psychological energy.

Deepening intimacy thins the Plexiglas and risks letting the true self be seen which can be quite threatening. Loving someone with a lot of Plexiglas requires patience and the very gradual building of trust.

The experience of being openly treasured, when combined with being *sustained* by having basic survival needs met, is the earliest basis on which basic trust is established. The message is first conveyed to a baby through steady, calm holding; safe, wide-open gazing; and tender, safe, nonsexual touch. These actions on the part of the primary caregivers fall into the action category of cherishing and communicate "I welcome you just because you exist. You don't have to do a thing to earn or deserve my love. I'm glad you're here. My own heart (my own true self) has room for you, a place for you. You're safe with me." That's the essential message behind all treasuring behaviors towards a loved one, whatever the person's age.

It's inevitable that disappointments will soon come in the course of a baby's life, evidence that even the primary nurturer has other things to do in addition to just adoring and meeting their every need! And so in the natural course of even optimal parenting, a child's heart clothes itself somewhat against the upsets of life. But if there is enough evidence of being treasured amidst the upsets, the layers remain like plastic wrap surrounding the still soft heart, the still trusting and hopeful true self. They don't harden into Plexiglas.

"I treasure you" is also conveyed by the mood and vibes given off by the caregiver. Positive and negative emotional energy are contagious, and for a child who has no knowledge about the world beyond what's right here, right now, all of the caregiver's good or bad energy is taken to be information "about me." It's "a reflection on me." To a child, the caregiver's mood and attentiveness tells them whether they are good or bad in that caregiver's eyes. Consequently, while feeding, clothing, diapering, bathing, etc. are technically sustaining actions in my framework, the manner in which they are carried out conveys "I treasure you" or something less affirming than that, ranging from "you're not important" if the caregiver is thoroughly preoccupied or distracted, to "you're a bother" if the caregiver is upset about something. As I've said earlier, as adults, you and I know the preoccupation or sadness/frustration/anger, etc. of the caregiver may not be about the baby/child at all, but it's important to understand that the child's brain does not yet recognize the existence of a world beyond what their five senses take in, much less have the capacity to make sense of where they fit in the adult's much larger world. For a small child, everything that happens around them is perceived as about them. It's simply the nature of having a literally undeveloped brain.[3] All of our wishing that the child could see the bigger picture can't make it so.

Even the best of lives are full of hard knocks and children start experiencing that early on, some more than others. For many children, the arrival of a new sibling causes their first heartache, the first evidence that "I am not the center of the world." Layers of plastic wrap are pretty much universal to protect a slightly wounded heart, but extra layers are often added when the timing of family events is particularly unfortunate for a child's developmental needs. One client's parents opened an in-home daycare when he was quite young, vastly diluting the mother's ability to attune to and respond to his needs. For another client, the wounds began at around age one when her parents accepted the demanding responsibility for two teenage nieces who brought upheaval with them into the home for a couple of years.

Even the most knowledgeable and best-intentioned parents cannot orchestrate life to perfectly insulate their children from difficulties, and the fact is that learning they are not the center of the world is a good thing for children, so long as they continue to know they matter. If a child's life is dominated by physical and/or emotional pain that is in no way caused by the caregivers (for instance, the child suffers from illness or accidental injuries) and those caregivers remain a source of comfort and treasuring amidst the pain, the child's heart will probably remain tender and open to relationships. And if the wound, whatever it is, is helped to heal by continued experiences of being treasured and by new opportunities for the true self to grow in autonomy, initiative, and competencies, the plastic wrap doesn't get thick enough to harden the heart or make it unreachable.

The presence or absence of Plexiglas when a person reaches adulthood has a major impact on their ability to form lasting and fulfilling relationships. Since mutual love in friendship and in marriage requires taking each other fully into account, if one person's true self is not fully available to be known, attempts to love each other well will be derailed over and over again. A couple may marry and have children and they will do the best they can to love them well—to manifest care in Erikson's terms. And they will do their best to care for each other. But things will be amiss if there is Plexiglas. Sadly, there is a lot of Plexiglas around a lot of hearts in this world.

As I've said, to *feel* love for another person is the sometimes surprising realization that your own heart, your own sense of self, has somehow enlarged to include them. When that happens, they become part of your treasure in life and you want them to thrive just as surely as you, yourself, want to thrive. In fact, you somehow know that their thriving is essential to your own sense of well-being and fulfillment. This subjective reality makes self-giving on their behalf far easier for you than extending yourself out of a sense of duty or a moral imperative. Anytime you're currently experiencing another person as in your heart you are probably motivated to extend yourself for them.

> Friends recently took their little granddaughter to breakfast at a restaurant and before leaving, the grandmother took the jelly-smeared little girl to the restroom to clean her up a bit. Rather than quickly washing her face and hands so they could head out the door, my friend was amazed to find herself patiently responding to the "I want to do it myself" of this autonomy-seeking two-year-old. "I was never that patient with my sons at that age! I didn't have time!" she told me. Taking the necessary time, she let her granddaughter get her own paper towels, turn on the water and get them wet, and praised the little girl's competency in using the paper towels to clean her own face and hands. She encouraged her every step of the way and could see the joy of accomplishment on her granddaughter's face. Only a little while later in the grocery store, out of nowhere, the child beamed up at her from the shopping cart and said with exuberance "I wuv you, Grammy!" This little girl's love tank was clearly overflowing from the evidence that she mattered and that Grammy treasures her.

Being treasured by parents and *knowing* it is the ideal garden environment in which to grow. When being treasured is the air you breathe, the various prunings, repottings, rainstorms and droughts, etc. can usually be handled relatively well. Experiencing this early in life can set the stage for fairly easily believing you matter to others as you grow up and opens the way for friendships characterized by treasuring, as well friendships that contribute greatly to the development of the ego strengths. Emily writes of such a friendship and how it has helped her grow:

> My best friend and I have treasured each other since we were four and we're now sharing an apartment. Her mother babysat me and my brother and we became like sisters; we had our share of fights, but always had the most fun when we were together in our own little world. Toward the end of grade school, she moved out of state and although we remained friends through notes and short visits, it didn't feel the same. But four years later, just as high school began, she moved back and it was as if she'd never left. We've messed up and had our fights, but we've always been able to forgive each other. We can be honest with each other about what we think and not have it held against us. She's always been there for me, supporting me even when it's hard. Late-night calls always end with "I love you and it'll be okay." I don't think either of us has really thought of this as a love relationship, but it is. Our friendship has pushed me to do things I wasn't sure I could handle and reach goals I thought I wasn't capable of. She has helped me with purpose, competence, fidelity, and mutuality, giving me courage to pursue and complete personal goals, and we've learned how to care for each other. No matter what happens, we will always be there for each other.

As Emily's reflections make clear, when a person securely knows they are treasured, they're more able to listen to the kind of honest feedback that may be hard to hear. This degree of trust is what allows a love relationship to be such a powerful instrument of positive transformation in a person's life. (It's also what makes betrayal of that trust so devastating when it happens, but that's not our focus here.)

There are people who treasure deeply but don't show it, either through embarrassment, fear, or just not knowing how. If your loved one doesn't know you treasure them, their Matter Meter registers on the low side and little refreshment for the journey is being added to their water tank. Like it or not, a recipient of your actions doesn't know your motivation for sustaining, supporting, etc. unless you reveal it to them through the actions I'll describe in the next chapter. You can hope it's obvious all you want to and that doesn't change that fact that you evidently haven't acted in ways that effectively convey "You're part of my treasure in life." Individuals who lost touch early in their own lives with this need to have it clearly conveyed to them through actions have a tendency to discount its importance to others and even to belittle it, making matters even worse in their relationship.

Also, if you've fallen into the rut of not communicating your treasuring for a long time, thinking it should be good enough that you expressed it in the past, you might want to rethink that assumption. Like it or not, the slow grind of being taken for granted can erode a loved one's earlier knowledge of being treasured. Feeling gratitude is a hallmark of treasuring someone, so if you find yourself taking that person for granted, consider this a flashing yellow caution light. If it's been a while since you displayed evidence of treasuring directly to your loved one, whether it's a child, friend, spouse, or parent, you might want to pay close attention to the next chapter.

6

Love Nurtures by Actively Cherishing a Loved One

Some people are amazed to realize that they have let someone into their heart. If they have never experienced being cherished as evidence of being treasured, it surprises them to discover the protective barriers around their heart can let another person in. People describe it variously as melting, the walls collapsing, or like a door or window opening in their heart. Several years ago, I was working with a middle-aged couple separately on their marriage, trying to help them reopen their hearts to each other after years of inflicting wounds and being guarded. In a session with the husband, I described my image of building up thin or thick Plexiglas walls around our hearts. He suddenly remembered the moment when he had held his newborn daughter and gazed into her eyes and fallen in love with her. He told me his heart had broken open in wonder and awe in those moments and it provided him a reference point for realizing how high and thick and guarded the walls around his heart had become with his wife. It also gave him a vivid image of what he was up against if he wanted her to eventually let him back into *her* heart. He could understand my goal of restoring enough safety in the marriage to thin those protective layers a little at a time until each could risk letting the other feel the softness of their heart again.

Others are amazed in adulthood to discover they have a place in someone *else's* heart. One of the first times I taught this material to a class of college students, a young woman who was a single mom had to drop out a few weeks into the semester, just after we had covered my framework. Anna's life settled down enough to return to school a year or so later, and she reenrolled in the class. In her final paper, she wrote:

> I hadn't heard of treasuring until I took your class the first time. It sounded nice, so ideal, and it's how I felt toward my children. They are my world and some days I just watch them and marvel. But the idea of someone feeling that way about me was foreign. The idea of being in a relationship with someone who loved me simply for who I am seemed impossible. And then I met Keith (so different from her ex-fiancé, father of one of her children). We talk about everything and when we run out of things to say we just sit there smiling at each other. We just make each other happy, just being ourselves. The incident that felt so treasuring will probably seem inconsequential to you, as it did to him until I explained it. One day last winter, we had a heavy snow and after getting the kids up and moving, I went out to shovel the driveway, clean the car off, and take the trash out. To my surprise, these things had already been done for me. Keith had gotten up hours earlier just to come to my house and do these things because he knew how hectic my mornings already are. When he came over later, I cried like a baby because I finally realized how much he cared for me. I'd never had anyone want to help me or take care of me before and it felt so nice to be cared for.

Anna's childhood had not afforded her the emotional safety of being treasured, and she had not consciously looked for it in a boyfriend. The genuine love this man offered in contrast to what she had settled for in her earlier relationships had made the words of my framework come alive for her. Cherishing actions of mutual gazing and emotionally intimate sharing with minimal

Plexiglas had been establishing the truth of his love for her. In that context, the unexpected act of service touched her deeply, strengthening her hope that reliable love might be a reality in her own life.

Another student, Martha, described how the treasuring experienced in a college friendship had helped provide a later-in-life repair for something that had been lacking in her early years:

> I was residence assistant in my dorm. Sally's outgoing personality and bubbly laughter spread throughout the floor that year, creating a community that I don't think would have been present without her. She was classified as "Mama Sally" by many of the residents because she always had Band-Aids, aspirin, great advice, and a knack for listening. This first year of college was the start of treasure love between Sally and me. (Growing during the first three years of school, Martha says their treasuring for each other is shown through being there in times of need, at family events, helping each other, and just being supportive.) We feel safe, secure, and are there for each other—no matter what.

One of the themes that comes up often as students write about having been treasured by someone is dependability: "They were always there for me." No matter what mess they'd gotten into, no matter what stupid mistakes they had made, no matter how disappointed the person was with them—that person was still "there for me when I needed them." These life-affirming connections that prove the care isn't conditional on measuring up put water-for-the-journey into that inner tank.

From an early age, Carrie was in the primary custody of her mother, a woman who could not make herself leave the relationship with an abusive boyfriend. Carrie spent every other weekend with her father and stepmother, and during the rest of the time, she bounced with her mother from the houses of a current boyfriend to various havens provided by friends and relatives. She doesn't know what empowered her at the age of five to ask her mother to let her live primarily with her dad and stepmom, but the change provided a new beginning for her. Whereas basic trust and autonomy had been impossible to develop in the climate of her first five years, important reparative work began when she made the move. Carrie wrote of her stepmother's dependability and its impact on her:

> It was Beth who was able to work with me through Erikson's stages of trust versus mistrust, and autonomy versus shame and self-doubt. I received sustaining nurture love from Beth from the day I moved in. Just because; I didn't have to earn it. Starting on that warm sunny day that I moved in and until the day that I am no longer here, Beth will continuously take care of me, whether I want it or not. Even now that I am almost twenty-three years old, she is aware of what it is that I need, want, and sometimes feel—even if I may not know it myself. (In my years with Beth and my father) I was able to catch up and grow and develop through Erikson's stages at a more normal rate. With a stable relationship with adult figures and no abuse, I was able to develop purpose and competence. Also, Beth's daycare allowed me the opportunity to interact with children of my age, teaching me age-appropriate play and how to build relationships.

Although she continued to have to spend weekends in the abusive situation in which her mother seemed trapped, with Beth's dependable help Carrie matured beyond her mother's emotional maturity level. At sixteen she was able to take a firm stand for herself and become emancipated.

For those of us who grew up being openly cherished, the in-person behaviors by which people convey treasuring seem very obvious, but they are a mystery and may feel awkward to many people who grew up without them. Because these actions sometimes communicate the love giver's deeply intimate experience of feeling connected, they can frighten a recipient who hasn't experienced it and doesn't understand it. They can be especially frightening to someone who was hurt or betrayed by inappropriate physical intimacy earlier in life, either by someone who was careless with or abused the privilege of closeness.

Cherishing actions are what create a secure attachment early in a relationship, especially with infants and children. Most cherishing throughout life begins and puts down at least the initial roots "in person", and that's an absolute requirement for infants and toddlers since their immature brains literally do not comprehend another's existence apart from physical presence. Once the seed is planted, an older child, teenager, or adult can experience the growth and maintenance of cherishing through telephone calls, video chats, self-revealing letters and e-mails, as well as other actions identified by Gary Chapman in his work on love languages.[1] Acts of service and insightful gifts—two of Chapman's categories—can certainly deepen the recipient's belief that they have a place in the giver's heart. Let's look at some of the cherishing actions that plant seeds and nourish the knowledge of "I'm treasured."

Mutual Gazing

The father I mentioned above as falling in love with his newborn daughter identified one of the hallmark actions of cherishing: mutual gazing. The poetic truth that the eyes are the windows to the soul is powerful. Now I'll grant you a newborn's eyes may not really be able to focus in the truest sense of that word, but that dad's inner experience was of each of them looking through wide-open windows into each other's unguarded souls, and he felt a communion that blew him away. That same unveiled mutual gazing is part of being in love wherein each person marvels at the wonder of feeling so open to and deeply connected with the other. Filmmakers often capture this meaningful look passing between people, a dropping of the veils that usually disguise or minimize what we reveal to others through our eyes. Films most often portray this intimate look between romantic lovers or soon-to-be-lovers, but the look I'm talking about is not primarily sexual and does not convey the lust of sexual appetite. It is a communion between two souls. One of the best film portrayals I've seen of this reality is the look that passes between Frodo and Sam near the conclusion of the movie version of *The Lord of the Rings* trilogy when Frodo is reunited with his companions. The science fiction film *Avatar* articulates well the importance and meaning of such unveiled eye contact when Jake learns from Natira that "I see you" in her culture really means "I see *into* you," into your innermost being.

Sustained unveiled eye contact between people is an intimate experience, one which can feel very threatening if you don't *want* to be seen and known. Therefore, it is an indication of trust when two people allow it to happen between them without quickly putting up veils to diffuse the intimacy. It conveys "I want to know who you really are, and I want you to know who I really am. I *want* us to matter to each other. I want us to be close." As with nonsexual holding discussed below, it can morph into or awaken in the recipient a look that conveys "I want you sexually," but it doesn't have to and, in fact, most of the time it shouldn't. Letting lust move on like a passing wave so that both people can drink *in* (imbibe) the reality of the nonsexual treasuring between them fills love tanks in a way that sex does not.

In Anna's case above, it was a combination of time spent talking about any and everything (intimacy), "just sitting there smiling at each other" (mutual gazing), topped off by Keith's acts of service that made it all sink in that she really mattered to him. This evidence of his treasuring poured abundant supplies into her tank. For Martha and Carrie, it was dependability that registered on the Matter Meter and refilled their tanks. These ways of "being there for me" came after many person-to-person interactions, all of them combining to established the truth of "I matter to you."

NONSEXUAL HOLDING

There are other specific behaviors that unmistakably give the message "you matter to me" and "I have a place for you in my heart." When an adult holds an infant or child close in a relaxed, secure way and stops all the busyness to just *be* together, their body rhythms synchronize and an amazing sense of connection can grow between them. They both drink during such times, that is, water flows into the tank. As toddlers grow into bigger and more active children, these times happen less often, but many parents make an important ritual out of snuggling with their child at bedtime. Whether it's on the sofa together, in the big stuffed chair, or on the child's bed, these story times and/or conversation times are prime occasions for physical cherishing that conveys the inner reality of treasuring each other. As children get older and the physical snuggling becomes less appealing, lying on the bed beside them or sitting on the floor and leaning up against the bed after they're tucked in and the lights are dim can create the opportunity for more intimate conversations about what's going on in their world. Yes, children often try to stay up later by doing this and it can get out of hand, but there is great value in the message of cherishing that comes through these bedtime conversations together, and adults do well to build them in to the healthy timeframe.

Tammy described a relationship with her grandparents in which she knew she was treasured, a relationship that has contributed to developing basic trust:

> As a ritual every night, I would crawl into my grandparents' large four-poster bed and listen intently to the stories that came. I could always count on the land of fantasy to fill my head as I would drift off to sleep. My grandmother would come up with wonderful stories of wild trips to the moon in a barber chair to get our hair done. She would continue entertaining my childhood imagination while rubbing my back until I fell peacefully asleep. Then it was my grandfather's duty to carry me into my room, saying "I love you, Tammy," and then tuck me in for the night. I have always felt safe in their home.

Tammy's example reminded me that after my grandmother moved in with us when I was ten, well into my teen years I would lay down on her big bed with her after dinner and spend time watching her favorite television shows, resting in her comfortable presence and basking in the reality that we treasured each other and enjoyed the closeness of each other's presence.

Between older children who become friends, older children and adults, and between many adults, there continue to be physical behaviors that set a treasured person apart from how we relate to other people. For one thing, we more readily allow them into our personal space. Children who love each other hold hands unself-consciously, sit practically on top of each other, and even teenage girls love forming what I call puppy piles because they relish the closeness. Female brains, in particular, release oxytocin (a feel-good, calming chemical in the brain) during nonsexual snuggling as well as during positive emotional interactions and intimate conversations, so the emotional bonds between adolescent girls create a craving for those kinds of contact with each other. Girls sometimes confuse these longings with sexual longings and during those confusing years after puberty, sexual identity confusion can create a lot of anxiety and a lot of experimenting. It's important to understand that not all physical attraction is sexual in origin or goal. We are part of the family of mammals and we long for touch, some of us more than others. Our brains reinforce the experience of safe physical closeness with feel-good chemicals.

Typically, we're more naturally inclined to touch people we treasure, and we hold them longer when we hug—if we let ourselves. Experiments on hugging show that a twenty-second hold/embrace (with someone from whom you welcome it) rather than a quick hug triggers the brain to release oxytocin. [2] Cultures vary as to what's socially acceptable across the sexes and within the sexes. In many nonwestern cultures, adult friends of the same gender hold hands without anyone imputing a sexual bond between them; it is simply an expression of cherishing each other in deep friendship. So please remember that I'm discussing physical touch that is completely innocent and nonsexual, regardless of the sex of the people involved.

> Peggy tells about a relationship of three-and-a-half years in which she experienced this gift of nonsexual holding at a time she was in tremendous emotional pain. Finishing her senior year requirements had exhausted her. The absence of her recently deceased mother from the graduation ceremony had been wrenching, and her father's new romantic relationship had added to her emotional stress. She had felt close to breaking down and when she went to her boyfriend's place, the walls came down and the tears came. "I was embarrassed and ashamed, and he was a little confused at first. But then he did something that to this day still surprises me. He took me into his arms and just held me. He gave me that condition-free, cherishing, safe treasuring Nurture Love that I needed. He was there to soothe me, understand me, and accept me. He held me for a long time and while it definitely didn't make things go away, in those moments it made everything a little more okay.

In many cases, physical expressions of cherishing change over the duration of relationships, often with males becoming less touchy-feely as time goes by. It bears repeating that throughout life, the female brain naturally releases a lot more oxytocin with snuggling, hand-holding, tender eye contact and meaningful conversation than typical male brains do. That means females get a bigger payoff for nonsexual physical touch than males and, as a result, naturally seek it out more. When a male is in love, his brain chemistry responds to these physical expressions of love more like that of a female's brain, overriding the male's more typical lone-ranger approach to physical affection. Therefore, a woman may get the impression: He's a touchy-feely kind of guy. But when that phase of the relationship passes and his brain goes back to being more typically male, there's no natural chemical reward reinforcing the snuggling and physical closeness for him and it may largely disappear from his repertoire if he attends only to his own personal desires. The positive feedback from the loved one who does enjoy it may be enough to keep him at it, especially if he understands the importance of taking her needs into account. Since women typically continue to get a feel-good oxytocin release and to enjoy those cherishing behaviors, and since their man was quite forthcoming in the early phases, women often interpret these changes as a sign her place in his heart has diminished. If devotion is not actively replacing infatuation in the man's mind and heart, the relationship really *may* be moving onto shaky ground, but that isn't necessarily the case. Men who do treasure their wives and want them to continue feeling secure in that knowledge would do well to understanding this brain chemistry difference and make a point of actively cherishing the women they love.

I recently saw a brief scene at the end of a popular sitcom that captured it well. The fully dressed man and wife were on top of the bed, he stretched out and she cuddled up, her back to his front. She was telling him that when she's upset, she doesn't need him to solve it—just to listen and to wrap his big arms around her and hold her. As she nestled down to "drink in" his comforting presence, he reached up with the remote in his free hand and silently changed the channel of the muted television as his gaze lifted to the TV. Softly, and in disappointed disbelief, she said "really?" and as the credits came up, we heard the canned laughter of an audience in on the joke about men and women. Figuratively speaking, he evidently hoped she'd be able to drink even if he turned off the faucet. It's important to understand that for the comforting love to flow, the doors have to be simultaneously open to both people's hearts. Interestingly enough, if one falls asleep *but leaves the door open*, the other may be able to continue savoring the closeness. Or if one awakens before the other, but the doors of their hearts were open when they fell asleep, the awakened one can drink from the presence of the other. It's when one person's attention turns elsewhere that the flow of connecting energies stops.

Holding hands when out in public is a simply form of nonsexual touch that conveys two important messages: I enjoy being in physical touch with you *and* I'm comfortable with the world knowing we have a close connection. It's a low-intensity form of cherishing that simply keeps alive and well the message "you have a place in my heart."

I live in Maine now, and New Englanders are known for *not* indulging in physical displays of affection. This is in major contrast to the southern culture of Virginia where I grew up where we hug and kiss when we arrive and when we leave—and sometimes in between when there's emotional sharing of some kind! One New England student returning to college in midlife shared her delight that her teenagers would show their love for her in public:

> Most teenagers and young adults don't even want to be seen with their mom, much less be willing to show affection in public. My children, however, including my fifteen-year-old son run up to me and hug me in the grocery store

when they're out with their friends, even if they're going to see me at home in an hour. I feel cherished by them.

So keep in mind that the need for physical touch and prolonged holding between mammals meets physical and deep emotional needs that have nothing to do with sexuality and lust. It's true that nonsexual holding can cross over into activating sexual appetite, but the two are part of different action systems.[3] Children whose need for physical cherishing in early life goes unmet by parents or other caregivers are prone to begin at some point hoping and believing sex will be the answer. When these two action systems become glued together this way early in life, it can overburden the widespread marital challenge of managing unequal sex drives. In addition to the physiological incentive created in females by the oxytocin factor which I discussed earlier, teenagers of both sexes venturing into the world of intimate emotional and physical relationships sometimes develop intense attachments (crushes) on members of their same sex, often but not necessarily on individuals a bit older whom they look up to and admire. Sometimes they misinterpret these intense relationships and longings as evidence of homosexuality without ever being told that such intense identification and cherishing can be a normal part of a person's journey of sorting out who they are and who they want to be. In psychological terms, it could be called "falling in love with the ideal self."

These experiences are rarely acknowledged or discussed because sexual orientation issues have become so highly charged in recent years. It has become politically incorrect to discuss sexual identity confusion and experimentation as a fairly widespread phase many teens and young adults pass through since to interpret it as a phase is regarded as implying same-sex orientation and behavior can and should always be outgrown. One unfortunate consequence of the heated arguments about civil rights for same-sex couples is that information about this fairly common crossover from one action system (attachment) to another (lust and reproduction) is almost nonexistent in the popular culture. Scarcity of this information has consequences far beyond the labeling or mislabeling of one's sexual orientation. Confused and misguided teenagers, lacking in impulse control, too often sexually experiment with children or more naïve teens. In addition, many adults whose tenderness toward a child or teen turns into arousal fail to take responsibility for knowing the difference and disciplining their sexual appetites.

Even within marriages, this *crossover* of action systems causes more than a little unhappiness and conflict in couples when one person's hunger for snuggling only (i.e., to satisfy and enjoy attachment and express cherishing) activates the other's sexual appetite. Couples who recognize the difference, find ways to communicate clearly, and take both types of need into account have more stable relationships than those who continually misread each other or proceed at cross purposes.

Unfortunately, we are currently in an era in American culture when sexual touch and fulfillment of each other's sexual desires has been separated from cherishing in the minds and value systems of many people. Personally, I'm old-fashioned and believe that a consummated sexual relationship belongs only in a relationship in which both people do have a place in each other's hearts. Even if you disagree with me on this point, my other observations about the Nurture Loves and Challenge Loves still hold true.

There is no shortage of books promoting healthy expression of our sexuality, so I need only acknowledge here that sexual touch is an important expression of treasuring within some relationships. My own concern is to draw attention to the underrecognized importance of completely nonsexual physical touch that conveys "I treasure you. Physical contact and holding you close gives me deep contentment." Safe, tenderhearted touch and holding for its own sake and not with an ulterior motive of sex creates a secure bond, whatever the age, and helps that bond last.

Carol J. Sherman, PhD

Time *With* a Loved One

How we spend our time is another physical indication of who or what we treasure and this is often a source of misunderstanding in relationships. When we spend time with someone we treasure, we might both be engaged in an activity we both enjoy equally. Sometimes, however, we take part in an activity primarily because the person we love enjoys it so much and wants to share it with us. My husband's love of fly-fishing falls into this category. Myself? I love surf fishing off the coast of North Carolina. Give me a nine-foot rig with real bait and a two-ounce sinker I can heave out beyond the breakers, and I'm in heaven standing there watching the waves roll in. When we moved to Maine, my husband gave L. L. Bean some business and took up this vastly different sport practiced on quiet lakes, out-of-the-way streams, and off rugged river banks. It's something he can and does do on his own or with the guys, but going fly-fishing with him is one of the ways I cherish him because for him, that's quality time. I've learned to deal with lightweight fly rods and tiny fake insects that weigh nothing and which you have to try and flick into just the right spots where a fish is likely to be lurking. I do enjoy the settings, but I'm still more likely to land a shrub on the backcast than a brook trout or a salmon from the water. On the flip side, knowing how much I enjoy relatively low-exertion ways of spending time on coastal and lake waters, he recently ushered us into kayaking. (The gear-giving opportunities also solved his Christmas and birthday decisions for a while!)

Making and taking the time to be fully present with the loved one who needs to process an experience verbally or to be comforted or supported conveys "you matter to me" in ways that refill that person's tank. Chapman calls these experiences focused attention. One student wrote about her boyfriend:

> When I get emotional or upset, he comforts me and holds my hand rather than getting angry or annoyed. He sits there and listens to what I have to say. He not only listens,

but remembers things as well. A few days later, he asks me about the thing that upset me and if everything worked out. When he does that—not only listening, but remembering and asking me about it later—I feel like he truly cares about me and my well-being. I have never had this kind of love shown to me before and now I am beginning to develop the ego strength of intimacy and mutual love. The more he does things like this, the more love I show him in return. And love is so much better when both people are expressing it and feeling it.

Males have a poor reputation for being quietly present or for paying focused attention for more than a short time in emotion-laden conversations, so this example is particularly striking.

Spending Time *On* a Loved One

In addition to *time with*, we can also spend *time on* that person by doing things for them. This would show up in Chapman's acts of service. Sometimes it's time working with them to help them accomplish something such as when my older brother showed up at 11:00 p.m. to help me meet the midnight deadline for moving out of my apartment when I was in my twenties. At other times, you simply do a job for a loved one to take it off their plate, such as when Anna's boyfriend (above) cleared the foot of snow off her car so she'd have an easier departure for school. If we have eyes to see it, these acts of service are expressions of deep, abiding love.

Time Watching a Loved One's Display of Competencies

Inner treasuring is also conveyed outwardly when we spend time *witnessing* a loved one from the audience or sidelines while they do something that's important to them. As we'll see when we look more closely at supportive love, showing up at sporting events and school performances, etc. is an act of cherishing since it confirms the reality "You're a high priority—I treasure you."

And this doesn't apply just to parents and their children. When spouses and friends show up for each other's theater performances, concerts, recognition ceremonies, etc. it conveys "You matter to me." Once treasuring is well-established, attending all the events may not be necessary to convey this truth. But when a person is in doubt about their value to you, not showing up can cause leakage from the tank. "Surely it shouldn't matter to a mature adult," you may say, but the truth of the matter is, it does. Many times a child, spouse, or friend understands the competing responsibilities that keep us away, but even so, when we make the effort and do show up, it registers on the Matter Meter.

The Importance of Gratitude

Helen Fisher, PhD is a biological anthropologist who has become well-known for her studies of the relationship between lust, romance and attachment in human beings. Using sophisticated methods for studying brain chemistry and electrical activity, she has shown that the exhilaration, preoccupation and cravings of in loveness are practically indistinguishable in the brain from those of drug addiction. This is largely because people in love are caught up in brains hijacked by dopamine, one of the brain's primary pleasure chemicals. Perhaps the wearing off of the head-over-heels elation and tunnel vision is somewhat related to an addict's development of tolerance for a particular drug. Visit her website HelenFisher.com for an array of her articles, books, and videos.

Given that the "head over heels in love" stage can be expected to fade as our neurochemicals get back to normal, what are the implications for heartfelt treasuring? When there is a lot of liking as well as loving beneath and around the chemistry in the relationship, a solid friendship forms the core of lasting devotion to each other. Both people accept that the initial blaze created by the chemistry (like the initial campfire blaze created by fatwood) is going to pass and both choose to tend the fire and keep it going through contributing to each other's lives in the various ways I'm describing throughout this book.

If we can be honest with ourselves about it, it feels great to be in love and therefore we go out of our way to do things for the object of our devotion to keep that great situation alive. It may appear to us and to them that we're being selfless and generous and that we're fundamentally that kind of generous self-giving person. But if we peel back the layers, most of that generosity is at least as much about seeking our own happiness as seeking theirs. We want them to love us so they'll choose us! As time passes and the brain chemicals return to normal, love either matures into a true devotion to the other person's well-being or it doesn't. (Familiarity doesn't have to breed contempt, but it does reduce the dopamine rushes and the addictive cravings for the other person.) If a truly solid friendship establishes itself at the core of the relationship, a union based on knowing and being known (intimacy) where each promotes the other's well-being through Nurture Love and Challenge Love, a very different kind of reward system sets in and weaves a tapestry in which both feel embedded and by which both feel enriched. When this happens, deep appreciation and gratitude for the other's true self-giving in mutual partnership take up residence where addictive and euphoric brain chemicals formerly reigned.

Unfortunately, many people consciously or unconsciously treat the marriage vows as some kind of finish line to being on good behavior ("Phew… now I can stop trying so hard to impress them with my generous nature") instead of the beginning of the next lap in a long-distance event full of potential for their own maturation in learning how to love well. A high percentage of people drop out of the event these days, largely because one or both parties return to a self-centered way of life. Tending the fire is where the attitude of devotion comes in, that second strand of the rope I described in chapter 1 as love at its finest. Not surprisingly, devotion produces gratitude in the loved one unless the recipient is very self-centered and feels entitled to it or becomes careless, taking the relationship for granted. Devotion is a mind-set we have to consciously cultivate as the brain chemicals calm down.

Most ministers will tell you premarital counseling is notoriously ineffective in imparting wisdom since most couples are unable or unwilling to actually think about the advice being given or the concerns being raised. But a dear friend recently shared a piece of sterling marriage advice given by the chaplain at the Naval Academy thirty some years earlier. The chaplain turned to my friend and said, "Remember, you're not getting married to make *yourself* happy; you're getting married to make *her* happy." And then he turned to the bride-to-be and said, "Remember, you're not getting married to make *yourself* happy; you're getting married to make *him* happy." It turned out to be very good advice that has served them well for over thirty years.

Only a combination of gratitude for the well-intended love that does come, forgiveness for a spouse's failures to love in exactly the ways we'd like, and humility about our own lapses in loving well will create the kind of marriage in which people thrive.

I want to take a brief side trip for the sake of readers who may be in relationship with a very self-centered person, or who may have had a very self-centered parent. There are some people who believe the world does and should revolve only around them and their needs. For various reasons, such people are stuck in a developmental outlook that dominates a normal eighteen-month-old and which most people, thank goodness, outgrow by around age three. Unfortunately, people who remain stuck there become adults who feel entitled to the excessive self-giving of everyone around them. If a person feels entitled to something, they don't feel very grateful for it so these people are the exception to much of the guidance I'm giving in this book. Because their ability to love is one-sided rather than mutual, if you practice the lessons of this book as you try to love those people better, you are likely to be used even more thoroughly than in the past. Your partner will be delighted that your self-giving has become so much more attuned, but their internal issues will probably continue to blind them about how to love *you* better.

The unvarnished truth is that loving a self-absorbed person is an endless challenge, but it can help to at least recognize what you're dealing with. Other writers can help you with this, including Nina Brown's *Children of the Self-Absorbed: A Grown-up's Guide to Getting over Narcissistic Parents* or Behary, Young, and Siegel's *Disarming the Narcissist: Surviving and Thriving with the Self-Absorbed*. I just want to warn you that hoping for mutual love with a person who has a narcissistic personality disorder may be a losing battle. Of course, if you ask them to read this book, it's possible it might generate a useful conversation or two, though it's more likely they will feel wounded or angered by your suggestion that they read it.

In summary, actions that communicate the message "I cherish you" require time, personal presence, and enough attentiveness to create a sustained connection. If these are absent or if they disappear, basic trust in the relationship and hope about relationships in general will be minimal.

7

Love Nurtures by Sustaining the Loved One

It seems pretty obvious to say that if you love someone, you will do everything you can to help keep them alive and well. Since my goal in writing this primer is to take what's obvious to people who understand love well and spell it out for those who don't, it's important to describe this aspect of love, too. To understand the essence of sustaining Nurture Love just ask yourself: "What are the basics a baby needs to survive after it's born?"

- air;
- water;
- food;
- clothing appropriate for the environment;
- medical/nursing care if ill;
- protection from predators and dangers of any kind; and
- soothing human touch when afraid or lonely.[1]

It's not as straightforward as it might seem though, since parents often disagree on whether, how and for how long these assistances should be provided to a child. For instance, one parent (typically the mother) might hold and comfort a hurt child immediately and for a longer time, while the other (typically the father) might respond minimally and encourage the child to hop up and get back to whatever the child was doing.[2]

Differences in opinion aside, however, when you love someone, you want to participate in taking care of them in ways that seem appropriate and reasonable to you. You may not always be in the mood or have the energy to do so, and you may often have other things you'd rather do, but the underlying desire for the loved one to thrive never goes away and usually helps you overcome those obstacles. As I pointed out earlier, whether or not the recipient experiences your actions as evidence of love rather than duty or obligation will be determined by whether or not they believe you treasure them.

I've discovered that many adults who did feel treasured as children have taken most of their parents' sustaining actions for granted. Many of my clients as well as most of my friends confess that they never really appreciated their parents until they, themselves, had children to raise and realized how much sacrifice is involved in good parenting. Most of the college students I teach admit they've never recognized these behaviors of their parents as manifestations of love until looking through the lenses of my framework.

The manner in which you sustain your loved one should contribute to their development and exercise of autonomy/willpower, initiative/purpose, diligence/competencies, and emerging sense of identity/true selfhood. This means you'll let the ways you provide food to a child evolve from breast or bottle feeding to feeding themselves, then to helping prepare meals and cleaning up after them, then doing the grocery shopping and cooking for themselves and maybe for everyone else. It means that at some point, not only will you encourage a child to dress themselves and do their own laundry, but you'll let them choose their own clothes (even if you don't fully appreciate their taste at times!) and maybe as they get older, you'll even expect them to earn the money to buy them. It means you will initially be on duty protecting your child yourself or checking out the reliability of the people into whose care you entrust them. Then, as the child becomes older, you will gradually teach them how to make good decisions about their safety so that eventually, you (with fear and trembling) allow them to take the car and go off on their own without adult supervision. And maybe, as my parents did, you'll manage to silence your fears as your small-town daughter heads off alone to a faraway big city for graduate school.

Anyone who has been a parent knows there is no reliable instruction book and we do the best we can, making plenty of mistakes along the way. But if you let yourself be guided by the following ego-strengthening goals, you'll probably be on track:

- Foster autonomy and assertion of the will, letting them make their own mistakes (unless it would be really dangerous to do so).
- Communicate it's okay to be a separate self, different from you in what they want and how they want to go about things. (That's fostering initiative in contrast to making your child feel guilty for not being just like you and wanting what you want.)
- Encourage diligence and the development of new competencies as you encourage them to help sustain themselves.
- As much as possible and safe, let them explore their identity as they change the ways they increasingly take over sustaining themselves. (Who am I? What do I like? What do I believe in and why? What's important to me and why?)

When a person believes deep down that the person sustaining them is doing it out of devotion (i.e., it grows out of treasuring), the acts of sustaining can have the effect of putting water into the recipient's inner tank.

Carol J. Sherman, PhD

SOME EXAMPLES OF SUSTAINING BY PARENTS

Often an experience affects more than one ego strength, evident in Trish's story of how her mother handled the situation when, around age three, Trish ended up in a scary situation on a family skiing trip:

> I rode the chairlift with one of my mom's friends and forgot to get off when I was supposed to, so I ended up all the way at the top of the hill, too scared to go down by myself. My mom had to ski down the hill she was on, come back up to the top, and ski down with me. She ended up skiing down the hill with me in-between her legs!

Rather than shaming her for her mistake or her fear, her mother's handling of the situation encouraged the development of willpower and growing competence and self-confidence as she helped Trish believe she could make it down the mountain with help. Reflecting on the experience, Trish realized she had felt safe all the way down the slope and confident of her mother's treasuring love. Her mom's actions took care of her physically, but they also protected her emotionally against the self-doubt that could have taken hold in that experience.

Often, it's extended family who sustain us. Allison tells about the key role her grandmother played in her life:

> Both my parents worked, so as a child, I spent a lot of time with my grandmother, and she played a big part in raising me. When I was sick, she had a knack for taking care of me. She would come to our house to get me and a blanket and a pillow so I could sleep on her couch. She made sure I had enough ginger ale and crackers. And she always made sure she kept some tomato soup around because she knew I didn't like chicken noodle like everyone else.

Tamika provides a good description of how her parents' ways of sustaining her have changed over time to fit her changing developmental needs. By attuning to her growth needs, they have fit their help to her situation, challenging her to develop in young adulthood the autonomy, initiative, and competencies appropriate to her stage of life:

> In childhood, they provided me with basically everything: food, shelter, medicine, clothing, transportation, and so on. Many young adults in college live in apartments and dorms. However, my parents were able to invest in buying a house for me to live in while I am in college. They still provide me with medical care when I am sick, but I am in charge of paying the electricity, water, and cable bills. I also provide my own food, clothing, and so on. I still have some concrete needs from them, but I also have the need to become more independent and they are facilitating that.

Mick's reflections about his dad reveal that sustaining often requires sacrifices from parents facing challenging situations:

> When I was eighteen months old, my parents divorced, and my father was left with three children to raise—myself, my older brother, and sister. My father could have shipped us off to our mother—who didn't want us at the time—but he didn't. He had been working first shift, but changed to third shift to earn more money and free himself up to take care of us during the day. He would get my brother and sister ready for school in the mornings and stay home to take care of me. He put food on the table, clothing on our backs, a roof over our heads, and took care of us all the time. He was father and mother to us. It was a very hard time for him handling three of us, but he pulled it off and somehow made time for all of us. He was devoted to us.

And then there's Nancy, a retired woman in my church who was thoroughly enjoying life on her own with her puppy and freedom to come and go as she pleased when her adult daughter had a terrible automobile accident. Nancy dropped everything and drove across four states to be there with her and has devoted the last several years to caring for her daughter during the long convalescence and rehabilitation.

Life is also filled with opportunities to lovingly sustain people who are not family members. Roberta tells how her parents extended themselves to help her brother's friend when arguments with his own parents during high school led to his being kicked out of his home:

> They treated him as if he were part of our family. Even though he only stayed for six months, he definitely grew into the family. My parents fed him, clothed him, took him to the doctors, and even grounded him like their own child.

Roberta went on to reflect that watching her parents' devotion to this boy helped form within her the ego strength of fidelity to her own crystallizing values and identity. By extending themselves in this way to not only sustain her brother's friend, but also to discipline him and be trustworthy toward him, they demonstrated their core values in ways that had a profound impact on their own children as well as the boy in need. She went on to note the impact her parents' loving actions evidently had on the teenage boy:

> He learned what commitment was while in our home, and that he could rely on someone and make commitments back to them. He slowly started to regain stability while in our home and eventually moved back in with his mom and stepfather. When he got a job after high school, he paid my parents back for living expenses even though they never asked. (In my parents) he had finally found someone he could trust and confide in. It helped him mature.

Roberta's example of her parents extending themselves to a boy in need makes it clear that the world is a better place when people behave in loving ways towards individuals they don't necessarily treasure personally. As I noted earlier, compassion is love that moves us to sustain and support others, even strangers, in times of clear need.

My student Tim reflected on the impact his church community had on him and his family by sustaining and supporting them when his little brother was born with a life-threatening condition:

> Every night during those first two weeks, someone from our church or neighborhood would leave a cooked meal in a Tupperware dish on our doorstep so that my mother and father would not have to worry about cooking food. It can be argued that the people from the church and our neighbors supported us for two reasons. One reason was because of feelings of love and attachment from the relationships we had built with them. The other reason was because of Christian values such as "love thy neighbor." Also people from the neighborhood constantly offered to babysit me while my parents went to the hospital two hours away to visit my baby brother. The sustaining love we received from the church greatly helped my family through this hard time.

Sustaining a loved one is often parent-to-child, but it can also be the other way around, as Stephanie recounts:

> As a single mom, I worked outside the home and was a full-time student. I came home at the end of the day exhausted to find the house clean and the evening meal prepared by my teenagers every day without being asked. After dinner, the children refused to allow me to clear the dishes, but insisted on cleaning the kitchen. My children were helping me grow by providing the safety of cherishing[3]... As a result of that love, I was developing the ego strength called identity, which is a feeling that you are somebody—you have an important role in the family. Even though they were taking over some of the duties that are typically a mom's responsibilities, I still felt valued and important in their lives.

Unfortunately, our feelings of love and our attitude of devotion can sometimes misguide us toward actions that don't really facilitate the well-being of the loved one. Sometimes this happens because we simply don't understand the ego strengths the loved one needs to acquire next. Or it can happen because we are too lazy to do the hard work of disciplining children. It can also happen because our own need to be liked dominates our approach to parenting. A very insightful student, Bob, provided the following example of a mother who nurtured and supported her children in ways that actually made them dependent rather than encouraging their development of core ego strengths:

> The mother washes all the clothes for all her children, gives them money whenever they ask for it (and even when they do not), and babies them whenever they want something done for them. Instead of getting them to do things on their own, they have learned to just get their mom to do it instead. This will cause many problems in the future because they will not know how to live on their own (and they may feel entitled for their spouses to do things for them as their mother has).

Bob's example points to one of the roots of entitlement: being spoiled by parents who have not loved in ways that bring about appropriate autonomy, initiative, and diligence in their children/teens as essential foundations for accepting responsibility for themselves. He notes that pampering breeds incompetence (which Erikson linked with inferiority) and having everything done for them fails to create purpose in them. In this case, the mother's care was misguided.

Mothers and fathers, single parents, godparents, grandparents, parents of friends, church members, neighbors, teenage children, adult children of aging parents, even (as in one client's life) the men or women who used to be married to one of our parents—people in these and so many other kinds of relationships show their love by sustaining us.

Sustaining in Marriage

In marriages that work well, couples mutually sustain each other, working out ways to share the responsibilities. Each arrives with a personal history of how the various sustaining jobs were carried out in their homes as they grew up. Assumptions, expectations, and often immature fantasies about "who's responsible for what" can fuel major tensions as a couple goes through the early practicing stage of becoming married. Add in the needs of a child or two and the picture can get pretty complex. It can be very hard to honor the commitment to attune—to take your spouse's needs into account as mattering just as much as your own as you work out these challenges—but that's the attitude you must bring to the discussion if you love the other person and not just yourself.

Protecting Others From Ourselves

One of the most important aspects of sustaining your loved ones is protecting them from *you*. One of the most widely acknowledged truths about marriage and family life is that our families—back at home behind the closed doors and windows of our homes—get our worst behaviors. "Everybody thinks my (mom, dad, son, daughter, brother, sister, grandmother, grandfather… *you fill in the blank*) is so (great, kind, polite, considerate, respectful… *you fill in the blank*), but at home, it's another story." It's as true of me as of anyone else. I make the effort to be my very best self when I'm at work, at church, in public. But when I get in the car with just my family or when I finally get home, it's as if a little switch goes off in my brain that says (in one of those computer voices), "You may now stop making the effort to be patient, polite, even-tempered, considerate, etc." Honestly, it's as if the little coaches and referees in our heads who keep us mostly abiding by the rules when we're in public go offline anytime we're with just our families—the people who are stuck with us. Even the best of us have to protect our families from this lazy streak in human nature.

Carol J. Sherman, PhD

It becomes a far more serious matter if we have aspects to our personality that we have trouble controlling: emotions, urges, addictions, or even illnesses that lead to erratic behaviors that can endanger our loved ones. I've known men and women who would never tolerate a stranger mistreating a member of their family, but who let their own anger or selfishness do great harm to the people they say they love. As I said earlier, I use the image of recognizing your temper, jealousy, sex drive, etc. as a small or large beast/monster/dog (choose your image) that you must put on a leash, tame, and train. It's simply not an option to let it keep pestering, frightening, biting, or otherwise harming your family. Again, this is too large a topic to address adequately here, but it's important to name it as a part of the sustaining behaviors of love.

The Challenge Loves

As I said in introducing part 4, if you love someone, not only do you delight in the fact they exist and make the effort to help them continue existing, but you also want them to grow and thrive emotionally, intellectually, psychologically, physically, socially, and spiritually. If you're attentive and attuned, you help them in appropriate ways to meet the challenges of life, whether those arise from internal changes or from the environment around them.

The hallmark of Challenge Love in action is participation in the loved one's interests and skill development—in short, in their pursuit of individuality separate from you but in relationship with you. It's what *they're* encountering as they grow, or it's their idea or interest, and it gives them satisfaction or joy. It may not affect you, the giver, directly at all, but because you have an attitude toward them of "I want to aid you in growing and thriving," you extend yourself to facilitate them anyway. Obviously, life circumstances limit how we can get involved, but we often have more freedom than we choose to exercise when it comes to being there for someone else. Children, teens, and adults are all keenly aware when people who say they love them seem to figure out ways to free up time for pursuits that are important to them personally, but can't seem to get free for the loved one's events.

If you love someone, obviously you hope they will want to remain an active part of your life, but real love isn't conditional on that requirement. The message of Challenge Love is "I'll help you learn to fly and then I'll hope I'm the kind of person with whom you'll want to remain in relationship." That's true of parents, friends, and spouses. When we love people well, they're more likely to freely choose to maintain a relationship with us out of enjoyment and gratitude rather than obligation.

For an action to qualify as Challenge Love, the giver must be attuned to the loved one and help them engage in interests and inclinations that are truly their own. You can make suggestions as part of introducing the loved one to new possibilities, but if you're encouraging or facilitating them to continue doing something that primarily gives *you* satisfaction, you're not really loving them, you're gratifying yourself. Way too many of my clients through the years have suspected or known that their dad or mom only supported their desire to play a musical instrument or a certain sport because the parent enjoyed it. A child does not feel supported in these situations, but instead feels pressured and (often) sad that their true self isn't being seen and encouraged.

> Mike loved baseball and was really good at it. His coach helped him become a really good pitcher. Mike's dad was a football fan, so Mike also played football since that's where he got recognition and support at home. When it came time for the baseball playoffs, the coach wanted Mike to pitch one of the key games, but his dad had weekend plans for the family which he refused to change and Mike missed his chance to shine. He always suspected that if it had been an opportunity to shine at football, his dad would have worked it out.

Undoubtedly, the father considered himself supportive of his son, but he was supporting his own passion so it didn't feel like love to his son. He lacked attunement to his son's true self.

When a child discovers they have to mold themselves to the parent's interest to get time, attention, and support, they will sometimes sacrifice their quest for purpose and competencies (i.e., they back away from exercising initiative as part of healthy separating) for the sake of preserving attachment. As noted earlier, they may develop a false (accommodating) self further as a way of gaining affirmation and relationship. Another client's father couldn't handle it if she beat him at pool as she got older and more skillful. She learned that if she wanted him to remain in a good mood and spend time with her, she had to secretly let him win. In adulthood, she still carries deep sadness about having to abandon herself this way for the sake of preserving the relationship.

Once children reach a certain age, they become pretty good at recognizing various disguises of self-love in their parents and siblings. The need for attachment, however, often wins out over the need for exercising the ego strengths and children/teens in these situations may turn down the voice of their true self to a whisper or even put it on mute. Many clients don't realize that their pervasive depression is really sadness felt by their abandoned true self who wasn't encouraged and supported, and eventually gave up.

As my students have pointed out, many instances of sustaining are experienced as support. And many instances of cherishing and support bring comfort and are therefore sustaining. The categories I have created are not hard, fast and rigid. Rather I have teased them apart to help you see that love in action has a direct impact on a loved one's acquisition of the components of resilience.

Let's look at the Challenge Loves at their best.

8

Challenge Love Supports the Loved One

When someone who matters to you is trying to accomplish something, there is a spectrum of ways for you to join them in meeting the challenge. Sometimes all they need from you is that you not interfere while at other times, if a hierarchy is involved, they may only need your permission. A loved one may need varying degrees of psychological, emotional, physical, and financial support as they pursue an interest or quest they've come up with on their own or one to which they have resigned themselves as part of a larger goal or value. It's unrealistic to think we can or should have a positive reaction to everything emerging in our loved one's personality or to all the things they want to be or do. For now, however, we're talking about traits and pursuits about which you are neutral or which you regard as good. (In chapter 11, I'll address those situations when you'd prefer to discourage, change, or stop a loved one rather than support them.)

These degrees of support include the following:

- openly encouraging them as they face the self-chosen or life-imposed challenge;
- witnessing their effort and cheering them on;

- facilitating them with transportation;
- facilitating them with equipment, uniforms, supplies, books, technology, fees, etc.; and
- assisting them in the actual doing, such as a parent helping with a science project, a brother helping select a car, a friend helping remodel a house, one spouse carrying extra financial responsibility during the other's schooling, an adult child helping her aging parent move from home to apartment to assisted living.

We'll look at each of these more closely and see some examples of support in action, along with how they can affect the acquisition of ego strengths, making the loved one's self more resilient. As you'll see in the examples, the actions overlap and double up, but I'll tease them apart to help you see the importance of each.

Love Supports by Encouraging

The most basic way to support a loved one is simply to encourage them. You cheer them on. If they goof up, you sympathize and boost their willingness to try again, emphasizing the value of learning from mistakes. For the moment, I'm confining this term *encourage* to the purely emotional and psychological realm because I want you to see that this has value in and of itself. When you're trying to love well, it can be important to insert a pause between encouraging and actively helping because the task itself may not be the most important thing going on. It may be that overcoming self-doubt, guilt, inferiority, or role confusion may be far more important in this particular situation than the consciously and publicly articulated objective. (These are the insufficiency sides of the toggles Erikson identified for those early stages. When a person's inner experience is dominated by these instead of their opposites—the ego strengths—the person tends to be far less effective in meeting life's challenges.)

For many adults, efficiency is often the top priority in any task, especially in our current culture that squeezes so many activities into whatever time is available. This pervasive focus on time efficiency can keep us from prioritizing the opportunities for fostering ego strengths inherent in a situation. Just a couple of days ago my husband, Bob, was part of a group of men and teens who gathered to build the stage at our church in preparation for the annual Christmas Eve pageant. When I asked how it had gone, he smiled and said it had taken a bit longer than strictly necessary because one of the dads had brought along his fifth and seventh grade sons who wanted to help with the power drills. As often happens on this leadership team, efficiency had taken a backseat to facilitating a new competency in these younger boys who were eager to get started in our youth mission program. Approaching tasks in a way that allows the time for promoting various ego strengths is an important part of a mentoring mind-set.

Fitting the support to the multiple needs of a loved one begins with noticing your baby trying to grasp something in their hands or trying to crawl. By your eager facial expression and tone of voice as you say "You can do it!" you show delight in their effort. When your toddler starts stacking blocks, you pay attention and cheer them on rather than doing it for them. When your six-year-old starts plinking on the piano, you may ask them to do it more quietly, but you invite them to make up a tune. When your fourteen-year-old comes home with a saxophone on loan from the band director, you encourage their practicing. When your fifteen-year-old tries out for the school play and gets a part, you offer to help them learn their lines.

And that's not all. Your manner of showing support has to fit the internal self-development needs of your loved one or your love won't be communicated. You may find it annoying and even unfair that it's not enough just to show up, provide the ride, buy the equipment, or help do the project. "I should still get credit for being there!" or "credit for helping," you insist. I'm just telling you the way it really is. If your tone of voice, facial expression, or body language conveys "This is a bother" or "I'd rather be elsewhere," it largely or completely cancels out any deposit into the love tank. (For instance, are you continually looking at your smartphone instead of the game or the stage when your child glances at you in the bleachers or in the audience?)

A young toddler climbing the slide at the playground is gaining courage and mastery; standing close enough to catch them if they fall is the action appropriate to their age and ability. You're supporting their initiative, autonomy, and development of a new competence by doing so and by offering verbal encouragement. If they lose their balance or take a tumble, you're by their side to minimize the damage. A middle schooler on the basketball court is also gaining mastery, but you have to be sensitive to the possibility that at this point in life, what may be more important is their investment in the separation work of adolescence. In other words, while they do need you to be there and available, if they get a bloody nose out on the court they probably need to demonstrate their separateness from you more than they need your nurture. Honoring their need for your presence at a distance is often part of loving them well at this stage. Again, you have to practice the skills of attunement and read their body language for guidance—and sometimes, if they're hard to read, you just have to ask them directly what would be most comfortable or important for them.

> Wanda described how her mother supported her as a small child. When it was time for preschool, her mom simply volunteered at the preschool where she could encourage her shy daughter with her presence. She didn't make a big deal of it, but simply helped her grow into the transition in a way that built more autonomy into her daughter's fledgling self.

While it's not true of everyone, most adults continue to thrive on the encouragement and emotional support from people who are important to them. Evidence that you've been paying enough attention to be aware of what's going on in their lives is like gentle rain that keeps them from getting so dried out and thirsty. When you listen to someone you love talk about challenges they're facing at work, in school, or in social relationships—and show you were really listening by checking back with them later about it—it's evidence they matter to you.

Carol J. Sherman, PhD

Our adult loved ones may also want to engage in activities that continue their mastery of new competencies, activities that involve separateness from us.

Love Witnesses and Affirms our Efforts

Encouragement moves to a stronger level when you spend your time showing up to witness your loved one doing whatever it is they're learning to do, or the things they simply enjoy doing, whatever the age. Children work hard to attain mastery of various kinds such as the following:

- singing in the chorus;
- acting in a play;
- playing an instrument in the band;
- spelling or doing math in a bee;
- learning the art of debate; and
- playing a sport.

Having the parent and other people important to them show up and see and hear their developing competency establishes the belief that "I matter" in a very concrete way.

Parents aren't the only family members whose encouragement makes a difference. Dave credits his brother with loving him toward success:

> My oldest brother, Chris, has always been my biggest fan and supporter. I remember one time in particular when I was ten or eleven and had decided to quit school because I had done badly on a test in some class. Despite the fact that I had failed at something, my brother was right there to encourage me to try again. He believed in me even when I failed and he sympathized with that, but at the same time he let me know that I should work harder in the future.

Nick had gone to a college a thousand miles away from his family, moving into a culture very different from his own where his ethnicity stuck out like a sore thumb. The support he needed came from his brother:

> Although I would never admit it to my close male friends, I was having a hard time adapting to the new lifestyle, and more than once I contemplated returning home. The only person I felt comfortable discussing my feelings about this with was my older brother. I remember one night in particular when I called him up and told him that I thought I was just going to come home. My brother told me that if I felt that was the only and best option for me, he would support me in that decision 100 percent. However, at that point, he threw in the "but." He told me he believed we both knew that what I was doing was going to work out just fine for me and that even though I was far from home, I would be okay. I knew deep down that he was right and even though I do still get homesick, I'm glad I decided to stay here and continue my education. I think he helped me a lot with solidifying my identity. I know who I am and what I'm good at.

It was Nick's confidence in his brother's 100 percent support—his trust in his brother's "You matter to me" treasuring love behind the support—that was so key here. Needing guidance and encouragement, he credits his brother with helping him figure out who he is, what he's good and bad at, and how to be loyal to people.

Grandparents are often in a wonderful position to encourage growth. Although Anna wasn't close to her father, her grandfather was the male she looked up to:

> He always pushed me to do well in school and would get so excited when I worked hard and earned good grades. Middle school was the first time when my school started giving out awards for doing well. Every marking period my grandfather would cut out the newspaper clipping that listed the names of kids who had made honor roll. He always highlighted my name and gave it to me, telling me what a good job I had done. This was during my school age years when I was struggling with industry vs. inferiority.

> My grandfather definitely helped me to better myself by encouraging me to work hard and showing me how proud he was of me.

In adulthood, marital partners continue to thrive on the encouragement of their spouses and families. It's important to have their competencies witnessed, especially when they accomplish something new to them. When adults perform in community theater or play in athletic leagues, it refills their tank to have family and friends show up to see their efforts and accomplishments. Adults who had plenty of this kind of support from parents are sometimes oblivious to how much a spouse who had little of it growing up wants this kind of encouragement and support in adulthood.

Love Facilitates

In addition to moral support (which has nothing to do with morals and everything to do with a person's morale!) by verbally encouraging and personally witnessing the person demonstrating their growing competence, there are ways of supporting the person tangibly, logistically, and financially. Again, the type of support and the manner in which it is given can squelch the development of ego strengths or boost them, and attunement is the best guide.

Here is a young student mother's reflection about the resilience she is seeing in her four-year-old:

> She is able to pick out her own clothes and get dressed all by herself. She is able to brush her teeth and her hair in the morning as well. She takes the initiative to get herself a snack if she is hungry instead of having me get it for her. This also motivates her to take initiative. She still has struggles at times and gets frustrated when she can't accomplish something herself, but I give her a little help and encouragement to keep her positive. This supporting love is encouraging her to develop autonomy.

To a parent who loves well and easily, this young mom's account may seem mundane, but there is a world of difference between this child's experience of being encouraged and facilitated and the memories one of my clients has of having to get himself dressed because his mother wasn't around very much and having to look in all the cabinets for something to eat.

Facilitating an older child interested in playing the flute might involve renting an instrument or paying for lessons—and then attending the recitals to witness and applaud what they've learned to do. Facilitating an adult friend might be loaning them a suit to wear to a big interview to help them look their best and boost their confidence.

Parents who have tried to support a child's interests may have a hard time letting it go when the child outgrows the pursuit or loses interest. But exploring parts of the self and having freedom to say "No, it's not really me" or "Yes, I loved it but it's not what I want to spend my life doing" are important aspects of discovering one's identity/true selfhood. Realistically, most parents have limited resources available for such experimentation, and this can be explained to a child—or a teen. And spouses should engage in a reality-check discussion when new yearnings appear in adulthood. Still, to the extent possible, people need opportunities to explore a new interest without feeling obligated to stay with it forever.

> Maddie tells how, as a child, she would sit in front of the mirror and put on makeup, do her hair, and pretend to be someone else. She'd have her siblings take pictures of her and tell her how beautiful she was. "It was a blast." Her parents noticed all this so they enrolled her in a modeling school. They made sacrifices to be able to afford this experience for her and they attended her shows. This schooling was a part of her identity/fidelity stage. They were not judgmental of her love for modeling and supported her in it, making it possible for her to go forward with it. In the process of attending the school, Maddie discovered

that spending her life as a model was not who she was. "My parents never stopped loving me after I told them that I didn't want to go on with modeling. They weren't mad about the money they'd spent, but were just happy I'd tried something I'd wanted to do."

Another student, Denise, captured well the way her parents' support morphed across the years:

> Through the years, I tried many different activities and involvements—basketball, softball, field hockey, among them. My parents drove me to practices and sat and watched my games. They were there to cheer me and watch me and notice when I did well. Later, I got more involved in academic clubs. I went to competitions and wrote for the school newspaper. While my parents couldn't be physically present to cheer me on for that, they would be there to drive me home after school if I stayed late. They always asked for a copy of the paper I wrote because they wanted to read my work, and whenever I did well at a competition, they congratulated me and showed me how proud they were of my success. My extracurricular activities at college have changed once again—to drama. Even if I'm not acting and am just a part of the stage crew, they attend and show their support. Their presence and active support through all these changes has helped me develop the ego strength of taking initiative to pursue things I enjoy or find satisfying.

As the identity search years move into full swing in adolescence, it can be very challenging for parents to figure out how to support their adolescents/young adults. Meg's account reveals some of those challenges and how her mom handled them:

> When growing up, it was my mom who knew me the best of anyone. We had a great relationship that resulted in her having good insight into who I was. Ever since I had gone to work with my mom, a registered nurse, I had

> known I wanted to go into the medical field. For a long time, what I wanted to be changed from day to day. For the longest time, I wanted to be a pharmacist. I could tell my mom wasn't fond of this idea. In retrospect, I realize my mom just realized this field was not something I was likely to enjoy. Instead of just outright telling me that, she just encouraged me to look into different medical field options. Over time, I ended up choosing physical therapy on my own after shadowing a physical therapist and doing a lot of research. During this whole process, my mom encouraged me to see my other options, but allowed me to make my own decision. I knew that if I still wanted to go into pharmacy, my mom would still support me; it was nice to have her guidance without feeling pushed.

Some parents believe that if their child doesn't get much playing time during games, there is no point in being on a team. It's not the case for all children/teens, but for some it's not excellence and a high degree of skill development that matters so much as the sense of belonging and a chance to develop social competencies.

> Lynn wanted to be athletic, like her brother. She liked running and wanted to be on a team even though she was not good enough to help the team take medals. "Mom was there cheering me on and giving me the confidence to at least keep trying, even though I knew I wasn't any good. Although I never won a trophy for it, I had fun on the track team all through school."

Love Actively Pitches in to Help

Sometimes it's difficult to keep from just taking over and mostly doing a project for a child who has bitten off a bit more than they can chew, especially if it isn't going well. I remember my excitement in fourth grade as I undertook to build a rather large model of a medieval castle out of corrugated cardboard for class. My father worked patiently to help me get the towers and walls cut out and taped together, but I remember his frustration as the cardboard soaked up one can of gray spray paint after another and still didn't look the way I wanted it to look. Money was tight in those days, and I seem to remember calling it "good" at the point when getting another can of paint was going to come out of my allowance! Another example comes from a good friend:

> Richard had spent a summer during high school working at a boatyard, learning to build and restore wooden boats. He used his savings to buy a very beat-up classic boat at a very good price and started restoring it on his own. It turned out to be a far more extensive undertaking than he had expected, but it was clear his skills were equal to the task and the outcome had a lot of potential. His mom worked with him to bring the job to completion and he was able to display the finished product to admiring potential buyers.

Often, in fact much of the time, love's actions blend sustaining with supporting and teaching. And the reality is that when it's hard, the recipient is more likely to realize the treasuring that's being expressed through it. After Peggy left her abusive fiance—the father of her small son and infant daughter—her mother was skeptical about her daughter's ability to pull off college under those circumstances. They discussed and debated for a couple of months before her mother decided to help her try:

> She helped me fill out my application for a professional program within the college and was shocked and proud when I received my acceptance letter less than a week after I sent in my application. From that point on, she believed I could do it. She helped me with the kids when I needed to study and made sure I had all the resources I needed so I could focus on school. Now, a year later, I have a new apartment attached to my parents' house, and I think that is the ultimate show of support, helping me 24/7, which I know is exhausting. By helping me go to school like I so badly wanted, and supporting me and letting me know that if I didn't do well I could always try later when the

> kids were older, my mother helped me begin to develop the strength of identity that I had been missing for so many years. I am now more confident and I believe that the decisions I make are the right ones. And while I still have some leftover quirks from my seven years of abuse, I'm much healthier and better off now that I'm in school. I feel like all those times I was told I was stupid are laughable now—because clearly, I'm not.

As life proceeds and we get into pair-bonding relationships, it can become a lot harder to support a loved one in pursuing their dreams, especially if it might lead them away from us. In Becky's account below, you will see an example of ego strengths being fostered amidst the anxiety of the adult version of an attachment-separation cycle described in chapter 3. A less secure young man might have played on Becky's self-doubt and her guilt about spending time apart. Instead, her boyfriend encouraged and supported her into further development and strengthening of her true self:

> I did not want to leave him, but I knew I had to go to school. He was great. He helped me with my college applications as well as helping me figure out what I would be good at. He encouraged me to experience college life even though it meant only seeing him on the weekends. This was a time in my life where I needed to figure out what I was going to do with my life. (Becky notes here that she was wrestling with whether or not she felt competent to go away to school. She was reexperiencing industry vs. inferiority in the context of her identity search and launching from home.) I needed to figure out what would make me competent within society, and my boyfriend was helping me to accomplish this. We needed to learn how to function and live without each other. This was a huge adjustment for both of us because we'd seen each other every day for the previous year. Even though my boyfriend may not have wanted me to go away, he still let me do

what I thought was right. He showed me love by letting me do my own things. He never once pressured me into staying or going. He let me make my own decision. I think his doing this made me a better person today. I may not have gone to school if he had pressured me to stay home. I was young and naïve, and I would have done what he wanted me to do.

In a similar story, Sandra wrote about her own ways of supporting her boyfriend's aspirations:

When I first began dating Ted, he often talked about his hopes of enlisting in the coast guard. As he began the required testing process, I encouraged him and helped him prepare by sharing some of the study methods I'd learned in college. I helped him study and affirmed him before and after the test. When he faced leaving for boot camp, he was afraid I wouldn't still be here after the two-month separation, but I have been encouraging him any way I can. I write letters every day, telling him how proud I am of him and that I love him. We both believe we have found the person we want to spend our life with. I believe my support is helping him focus on his dream and is strengthening his willpower to achieve his goals in life.

In summary, when someone matters to you, you pay attention to what they're trying to accomplish. If they want help and their pursuit is not obviously harmful in some way, if it is at all possible you find ways to help them do it. Sometimes it's just showing up and cheering for them as they do it. Sometimes, it's just letting them know that it's not going to end the relationship if they pursue it. At other times, it's actively providing supplies or helping with logistics. Active support is a powerful way of communicating the underlying attitude that you are devoted to their well-being and the fulfillment of their potentials and their life dreams.

9

Challenge Love Coaches/Teaches the Loved One

If someone who matters to you has an interest in something about which you have knowledge or skill, or if they need to master it because of a larger goal, you can actively share the knowledge or guide them in developing the skill. If they want that from you, they will receive it as love. If they don't want it from you for some reason—and there can be many—they will experience it as intrusive and even controlling. This is another place where the skills of attunement are essential.

Developmentally, there are times when someone needs the room for trial and error, for figuring something out by themselves, or finding a teacher other than you.

- Maybe autonomy is what they're most hungry for right now.
- Maybe the accomplishment of doing it alone or even demonstrating the ability to seek out a source or teacher that's not you is what they need most right now.
- Maybe they need to know you're okay with them being separate from you and pursuing something you're not involved in.

It's also possible your manner of teaching doesn't empower others, but your loved one doesn't know how to ask you to change your style. For now, we'll go forward on the assumption you've discerned—or found out by asking directly—that sharing your knowledge and skill will be welcomed.

By definition, those who teach or coach us in some way are helping us develop mastery—and mastering new knowledge or new skills builds a person's self-esteem, putting supplies into the tank and helping them consolidate identity. Many people who teach or coach to make a living are not personally invested in their students, but many others are. Students of any age can tell when they matter to the teacher or coach as a person, rather than being just part of their job assignment. Yes, being helped as an individual or a team member to excel to the point of victory promotes competency, and self-esteem grows with those kinds of success. But when a person (whether child, teen, or adult) is on the receiving side of a teacher/coach's heartfelt time and attention, basic trust and hope are strengthened at their core because they have experienced "I matter."

Alison credits her father and stepmother for helping her develop competencies and confidence from an early age:

> When I was five, Peggy and my dad enrolled me in T-ball, coming to every game and practice to watch. I soon enrolled in softball and started playing year-round. My parents would coach all of the teams I was on, taking time away from their jobs and lives to be there for me. I remember working in the backyard for hours upon hours on catching, throwing, and hitting. We would stay out until dark so that I could master my softball skills. I was encouraged to participate in any and all clinics that were offered within a two-hour drive of our house, and I took full advantage of that. I played softball year-round for seven years, dragging my parents and younger brother up and down the eastern side of the United States for games and tournaments. Without the time, dedication, support,

coaching, and encouragement from Peggy, I never would have continued to play softball. I learned to never give up on what you want, even if it is something that doesn't seem to be reachable at that point in time. I also learned teamwork and dedication.

Tina was raised by her father after her parents divorced. The account below reveals how a parent's joy in a child's accomplishment makes a deep impression and also shows that parents are teaching their children unintentionally all the time whether they intend it or not:

> My father was a coach to me in many different ways. At a young age, I started copying everything he would do just like any child. There was even a time when I was about six years old that I shaved my face with one my father's razors. Long story short, he had to teach me that little girls do not shave their faces! One of my fondest memories with my father is the day he taught me how to ride my bike. Although it probably took weeks to actually learn how to ride efficiently, there is one day that stands out for me. He would tell me to pedal fast and try to keep my balance, all the while holding on to my handle bars and running beside me. Before I had even realized it, he was letting go more and more, and I was going further and further without his hands on the bike. Next thing I knew, I was riding on my own. I remember turning and looking at my father's face as he stood there with excitement and exclaimed, "Look, Tina, you're pedaling all by yourself! You're doing great! Keep at it—slow and steady."

Sometimes it's siblings who extend themselves for us this way. Sam's parents weren't around much when he was growing up. They were working hard to sustain the family physically. "This put the older children in a situation of having to take the lead and be parental figures for us younger ones." Whereas his father encouraged him to have ambition in school, Sam wasn't really interested or motivated for schoolwork. His interest and dreams were for basketball, something his oldest sister did well:

> My sister would stay outside with me until all hours of the night, playing basketball with me and teaching me little things. She came to my community center games and when my coach couldn't show up, she stepped in and coached the team. That meant a great deal to me because she was a role model to me. I lacked that support from my parents because they only had time to facilitate the idea of my dreams, but never really had time to physically be there for me the way my sister was.

Sam went on to reflect on his sister's important contributions in the industry vs. inferiority realm, on helping him develop competence which gave him confidence:

> She helped me study in order to maintain good grades. She always made sure I dressed well. And the support that she gave me with basketball gave me confidence. Where I'm from, basketball is everything. It is what gives you respect among your peers and it's what paves the way for you to go to college. I owe many of my successes to my sister because she allowed me to develop that sense of industry that I needed to get out of the tough place that I grew up in.

Vanessa described her father's teaching love for her brother, shown as they worked together on the truck:

> When my brother, Pete, first got his truck, he would get my dad to change his oil, brake pads, and fix it whenever it would breakdown. Over time, my brother spent time with my dad while he was fixing the truck and he slowly started to pick up on how to work on it. My dad taught him how to change the oil, change brake pads, check all the fluids, and basically repair it when it broke down. While he was teaching Pete, the two bonded. Whenever anyone's car broke down, Pete and my dad would go out and fix

it together. This time was also when the two of them had their most intimate talks. My dad would give him advice on all sorts of topics, including girls. This is when the two of them connected most.

Clearly, Pete was in the identity search stage of life, and as his father spent time with him, he was learning more than new skills. He was also learning the value of reliability and presence as character traits to emulate. Pete experienced his father as trustworthy and a source of honest advice. The secure emotional environment was deepening basic trust as a stronger core of his identity.

Extended family members often play key roles in helping us develop ego strengths. Seth tells about his uncle who hired him as a farmhand when he was in the sixth grade and taught him how to be industrious in very concrete ways. Seth's father worked with computers and technology, and the contrast of learning to do the hands-on work of a farmer had a big impact on Seth:

> He always treated me like an employee when I was working, but made sure to treat me like a nephew when we weren't working. I think that is important. He is known for his honesty and his hard work. When he expected these things from me, he did a great job at modeling it. This helped me grow in trustworthiness and reliability. When you see someone actually doing what they expect of you, it really shows how trustworthy that person is. There were times that I was lazy and didn't work as hard as I should have, but I think he had faith that I would turn out to be a worthwhile employee. He had faith in my character and my overall work ethic, despite the blips in my record. I didn't realize it at the time, but what I was sorting out was whether I was going to be a hard worker and an honest, trustworthy person, or if I was going to be lazy and sacrifice my integrity for the easy road. It was important that I had a role model like my uncle to show me the way to go.

Members of the larger community, including school and church, play significant roles in many lives. Jim's pastor has played a key role in mentoring him into young adulthood:

> He has given me the freedom to express ideas in a way that very few people have let me do. This is a type of teaching love. He willingly spends time with me whenever I ask him, investing a lot of time and energy into my growth as a person. He has shown me many times that he can be trusted. He is very open and is willing to share his own struggles in order to gain my trust. He is a very nonjudgmental person. He has a way of modeling right from wrong without putting a judgment on the individual. (His pastor's self-revelation allows a mutual deepening of trust, a central ingredient in intimacy. Thus, in the midst of conversations central to Jim's sorting out of what matters to him, who he wants to be, and what he wants to do with his life, he is simultaneously gaining experience of developing intimacy, the ego strength central to the next stage.) Knowing that he sees me as having potential and as a person who is an individual able to grow and learn from experiences helps me feel confident going into the future. (As Jim experiences himself as worthy of his pastor's trust over time, he discovers within himself a faithfulness and loyalty which are core ego strengths of identity formation.)

Obviously, people in the formal role of teacher in our lives can love us in this way. While there are some teachers who simply go through the motions, many others genuinely care about their students and it is inevitable that sometimes they take a special interest. Natalie was the recipient of one such college professor's care:

> Since that very first class, my professor has pushed me a lot harder than I was used to. The C pluses and Bs weren't anywhere near what my potential was and though I didn't necessarily recognize this myself, he certainly did. He began tutoring me and helping me learn alternative ways

to study, take notes, and retain information that I would need to know in the future. In my third year, I fell upon some hard times personally and as a result, my grades slipped. This professor noticed and asked to speak to me after class. He told me I was perhaps one of the most intelligent students that he'd had the pleasure of teaching. He went on to tell me that whatever was going on in my life was important, but that I shouldn't let it hinder me from reaching my full potential. Once again, he coached me on ways to adequately balance things out and work on my time management in a way that made sense to me, and as a result my grades began to go back up. Later when I asked if he would write letters of recommendation for me he said, "Absolutely. Your work has far exceeded my expectations." Coming from such an intelligent man who had put very high expectations upon me, I was very flattered and inspired. Because of this professor, I am able to set very high goals for myself that may take a lot of extra work, knowing I can achieve them.

Natalie went on to reflect on how this teacher had affected her development of the ego strengths Erikson identified. Though chronologically in young adulthood, she sees herself as moving into the capacity for generativity and care that Erikson says mark healthy adult life. She credits her teacher's mentoring with motivating her to apply herself to her work which, in turn, developed her self-confidence. By investing in her development, he was also positively affecting her identity search by helping her believe she had the potential to pursue a life she might never have had the nerve to envision.

Not everyone recognizes this kind of involvement and investment as love, but when you grasp the term more broadly, it's clear that extending yourself for the well-being and advancement of another person really can make a huge difference in a life. And affecting that one life has ripple effects. Does it arise out of treasuring as I have described it? Sometimes yes, sometimes no. A teacher can teach without devotion and in that case, there's only one strand (action) of the braid that is love at its fullest. In Natalie's case, she experienced her teacher as particularly devoted to her—adding a second strand of the braid—and that second strand of mattering made a difference, repairing some earlier wounds and strengthening some resources left weak from earlier experiences in life.

Will played some sports, but was overweight and out of shape. When he made a personal decision to run, lift weights, and eat right, he found his mother to be a wonderful teacher and coach:

> My mother is already a marathon runner, participating in the Boston Marathon, Disney World Marathon, Maine Marathon, and more. When I decided to take up running and try to go every day, my mother gave me some very good advice. She told me to try to do two miles a day overall, but that because I was just starting out, to see how far I could run and then walk the rest. When it came to eating, she helped me out on what constitutes a healthy diet. She told me what were good and bad carbohydrates. She'd cook me dinners consisting of fruits and vegetables, good carbs, and lean meat. The most important thing she taught me was to cut down my portions; and that if I followed all of her steps, I would see the pounds just shed off. I started to run and lift weights every day and before I knew it, I was down to almost one hundred and ninety—down forty pounds with the help of my mother. Towards the end of the summer, there was a 10K race around our area. A 10K is about 6.2 miles and it would be the first race I would ever do. My mom ran the race with me, and obviously she was in better shape than me, but instead of trying to get a really good race time, she decided she would stay by my side and support me throughout the race. Right around the five-mile mark, I broke down and almost decided to walk the rest. My mother, being the dedicated coach that she was, wouldn't let me, and told me to pick up the pace and finish the mile. I dug down a little bit and completed the race with my mom's coaching. If she hadn't been in the

race to coach me throughout the six miles, I would never have learned to push myself and complete the race. My next goal is to run a marathon with my mom.

Jack shared an example of his brother spending a summer at home after graduating from college (instead of staying at his usual job) specifically to coach Jack's baseball team. He wanted to share with Jack what college baseball had taught him:

> The fact that he wanted to take a full summer off, and train me and coach my summer league baseball team says a lot about his devotion towards me and my goal of becoming a better baseball player. He would have me outside three times a day practicing for forty-five minutes to an hour on various fielding and hitting drills. If I got tired, he would push me in a positive way, telling me that if he could do the drill, then I could definitely do the drill. He always said that I was a better athlete than he was and more talented. I don't know if I ever believed that, but it influenced me to try harder to be as good as he was or even better. He was honest and forthcoming with his constructive insights, and after listening and doing what he said to do, I could see the improvements I was making. This gave me assurance he knew what he was talking about.

In retrospect, Jack realized his brother's investment of time and talent into the development of his skill conveyed "you matter" which does strengthen a person's hope. He was also developing more competency as he applied himself to the goal. Evidence of competence doubles back and strengthens a person's hope. It's particularly important to note that because Jack trusted that he mattered to his brother, he could receive and grow from the corrective feedback. As you will see in chapter 11 on "Confronting Respectfully," it's human nature to get defensive when criticized, but when a person knows deep down they are treasured by the person confronting them, it's more likely they will give the critique a fair hearing.

Yet another student found herself showing generative care while in her late teens and early twenties, the chronological years Erikson says are dominated by identity and intimacy issues. Hannah writes:

> I have a six-year-old cousin who has a serious physical disability. He has spina bifida and a minor case of autism, and is locked into his wheelchair for almost his whole life. He loves to crawl and move around on the floor, but there is a time and place for it. About two years ago, I began to use the skills I learned as a physical therapy aide at my local hospital to show him some ways to get up and around easier than he could before. I used the skills I had learned to help strengthen his muscles and get him moving with his braces and walker. Not only did he immediately take to the situation, but he actually called and wanted me to be around all the time. I didn't notice it while I was working with him, but not only did he learn the things I was teaching him, but he also began gaining his own little personality. Before I started working with him, he was a very quiet and shy child. After a few months of spending time with me, he picked up on my actions and mannerisms and became quite the chatterbox. He now loves to talk to people he has never met and it really intrigues many people to see that such a developmentally challenged individual can carry on such a great conversation. I was moving into the generativity stage, consolidating the ego strength of care for someone else. I'd never thought I could be so close to a person so far from my age. I took a lot of pride in knowing I had helped him blossom.

This example clearly shows that abilities Erikson identifies as typically becoming central later in life are already budding during the earlier years. The fact that this is true is just common sense—after all, a ten-year-old diapering and feeding their baby brother is already manifesting a capacity to care that's contributing to the baby's acquisition of trust. Erikson clearly explained that he was identifying periods of emerging prominence of the various potentials. Various factors like brain development, physical coordination, and life circumstances come together for the first time to create the perfect storm of opportunity for that ego strength to emerge, be practiced, and crystallize into an inner resource. It may be practiced at an earlier chronological age—witness Hannah's demonstration of care for her cousin—but the time will be ripe for care to fully blossom later in life.

Note that Hannah was also solidifying her experience of competency as she applied her budding physical therapy skill and that her identity as someone who helps others through these skills was also becoming more solid.

Grandparents can be wonderful sources of teaching love. In the example below, the freedom to talk about any and everything was contributing to a child's basic trust, and it is clear that Toni knew by the quality of their time together that her grandmother treasured her. At the same time, Toni was developing competence and the early seeds of identity:

> My grandmother is a painter. At a very young age, I had an interest in art and my grandmother picked up on that. When I was really young, she would make crafts with me like paper dolls and other things, and eventually it turned into drawing and painting lessons which I enjoyed. Throughout my school years, I would go to her house twice a week and paint in her studio. I remember the Christmas she bought me my own easel—I was ecstatic and still have it. My grandmother took so much time out of her days to paint with me and help me learn what she had learned herself about painting. It's one of her joys and something she is very proud of, and she has passed that down to me. We would listen to classical music and paint next to each other. She even brought me to different galleries and art shows. I was able to meet other painters and always felt like I had a special bond with her. Emotions and feelings flow while I'm painting, and I could talk to my grandmother about anything during those afternoons together painting.

Teaching and coaching can happen between peers as we see in the following lengthy example of Mary helping a classmate with math, a subject in which she had a weak history herself. Mary includes important reflections about making it safe for another person to learn from you by empathizing and being sensitive to inferiority feelings hovering close to the surface. Thus, she demonstrates attunement at its best:

> I hate math. I stink at math. I had tried to take it as a summer course so I could focus on it and do nothing but math. They made me take a pretest, and I aced the algebra part of it, but failed the basic math skills part. They told me if they let me into the class I would undoubtedly fail it, and that it wouldn't matter how hard I worked. Because I was getting behind on all the things related to math in college, I decided to take it and retake it if necessary. My friend Becky, also math incompetent, ended up in class with me. We made a pact to help each other get through the class.
>
> It turns out that being good at algebra and not basic match doesn't really hurt you. I had studied, read, and taken piles of notes, all to help me succeed in this algebra class. Along the way, I discovered that Becky is worse at math than I am because she doesn't get the algebra part. Quickly we discovered we had a few hours of downtime during our algebra days and found a quiet place to work on our problems. Becky gets frustrated and stressed very easily, and I have learned to explain things piece by piece to her and to go very slowly so I don't overwhelm her. When I'm teaching her how to do math, I am a different person. I am calm and patient. I wait for her to ask me things. I don't jump ahead. I am trying to let her learn it at her own speed instead of telling her it's easy so she should get it.
>
> As a result of my teaching, we both have high As in our math class. I have demonstrated the safety of empathy toward her, discovering how she learns best and using

this to help her, and I have seen her grow. She has gained diligence and competency just by being successful in this one class. She now realizes that if she puts the time in and finds someone who understands what she needs to learn and who will work with her, she can do it. She has also gained identity, going from someone who thought she could never pass this class to becoming confident that if challenged to do so, she can use these skills. I'm glad I could help her grow as a person, but I'm also grateful for what I learned about myself. It has been years since I've taught anyone other than my kids, but I used to be a ski guide for the visually impaired, which I'm hoping to start again this winter, and I also taught nondisabled kids how to ski and snowboard. I had forgotten what it was like to get to know someone's personality and attune myself to it in a way to help them better themselves.

As adults, it's rare to know the inside story of those with whom we relate. If we approach them with the intention of respecting their strengths and building them up in their weaknesses, we are showing they matter to us as individuals. Craig is a young adult whose story of being trained by a caring mentor once again shows how time, presence, and attunement nurture and challenge the potential of someone who matters to us:

> To get hired on to the fire department as a *call* firefighter, you don't have to have any experience with firefighting at all. At first all I could do was help out on the scene by changing bottles on Airpacks and getting tools for people. I wanted to do so much more. I wanted to run the Jaw of Life, go inside, and get on the roof and cut the ventilation hole. I wanted all of it. The captain recognized this desire in me and must have seen potential. He came in on his days off and used his personal time to get me Airpack certified and provide me one-on-one time with all the tools. He took me under his wing, so to speak. He works for the state Fire Training Corps and allowed me to go to several towns and participate in fire training exercises that

gave me the experience I needed to become an interior firefighter—one who can go inside a burning building, do search and rescue, climb ladders, and put myself into dangerous situations to help other people. He showed me the safe way to do things, and when I had questions, he always made me try things first. He didn't tell me how to do something. He said. "Figure it out" and then if I did it wrong, he showed me the safe and easier way. I have gained very valuable experiences that are unique and worthwhile to my career. Today, I'm a firefighter II, going to fire school next year. He has provided me with the skills, knowledge, and mind-set to help me make a difference in people's lives. He has shown me coaching love. He never judged what I did as a fireman. He gave me the tools I needed and simply told me to get the job done and that he had confidence in me. He established a trusting relationship that is still very strong today.

I want to tie things together by reflecting on this example a little more fully. The captain instilled confidence in Craig by helping him develop skills/competence. He invested personal time and energy in Craig's development of those skills. The acquisition of skills gives a person confidence to act autonomously and to apply the newly acquired abilities with purpose. All of this contributed to the formation of Craig's sense of self/identity as a person who was not only motivated to help others, but also capable of doing so. For his part, the captain was going further than just doing his job. By taking Craig under his wing, he was caring for this young man as well as caring for the larger community he would serve as a firefighter. Thus, in Erikson's terms, the captain was *being generative*. Erikson uses a term from the world of machinery with interacting gears—cogwheeling—to convey this interplay between one person's ego strengths and another's.

Opportunities for teaching and coaching are present in many arenas in our lives. When the recipient really matters to the teacher as a person, extending ourselves in these ways is a manifestation of love.

10

Challenge Love Pollinates with Insights, Perspective and Inspiration

Most of us are farsighted when it comes to understanding ourselves: we're too close to the object to see it as a whole or to see it clearly. Because of this, we often need help from someone who has a little distance, loves us enough to have been paying attention, and sees us without so much of the clutter that can leave us confused. The help may come in the form of simple observations of what they've noticed about us. At other times, someone who loves us enough to have been paying attention may share significant insights about what seems to make us tick, and that information may help things become more clear.

I liken this to the role of bees in pollinating fruit trees or vegetable plants. For those of you who may have forgotten the basics from science class, I'll give you a refresher. As my friend Dave found out the year a late frost zapped the blossoms, for an orchard to bear fruit, the blossoms have to still be alive and be on the trees when the bees show up. And as he found out another year, if the bee population is low for whatever reason, few blossoms will be pollinated and you won't get many apples that year either. In other words, if there are no bees at the opportune time, the apple blossoms don't receive the tiny flecks of pollen necessary to start apples growing.

The pollen itself and the timing are both important, making the analogy a good one for this manifestation of love. Sometimes in order to discover things about themselves, a child, teenager, or adult needs to receive someone else's perspective. Without it, they're just not able to be fruitful.

Occasionally, bringing the pollen of information or insight to another person is as accidental as an actual bee inadvertently carrying pollen on its wing from one flower to another as it dines on nectar. More often, however, it comes from paying attention to the loved one, being attuned, noticing things about them over time, and caring enough to want that person to be fulfilled.

Pollinating someone you care about isn't about trying to make them share *your* interests although sometimes it does happen that the loved one has a talent or interest akin to yours—which may be why you noticed. First and foremost, it's about simply sharing what you've noticed, offering it as a no-strings-attached observation or suggestion of something to explore. When it works, it inspires the recipient by bringing into focus something about themselves that has remained elusive.

> When Sam was at a standstill in college, perplexed about what he enjoyed enough or found interesting enough to study, his mother had a low-key conversation with him, sharing what she had noticed about him through the years. She pointed out a time when he had jumped into action to take care of his older brother when he had cut himself badly and no adult was at home. She recalled a time at a soccer game when he had quickly scooped up a child who had been knocked silly by a forceful wayward ball, rushing her to the medic. She mentioned other memories of him thinking on his feet. "You know, you might want to think about being a paramedic," she said. A couple of weeks later, after mulling it over and talking with others about it, he told his family he was changing his major to

prepare for some kind of work in emergency medicine. After being an emergency medical technician, he went on to become a paramedic and after a number of years, was hired to become part of the Life Flight crew.

For Sam, the pollen came in the form of his mother synthesizing what she had noticed and putting it altogether in a way he just hadn't been able to see for himself. At other times, it takes the simpler form of noticing an interest or gift and bringing the pollen of recognizing a good fit. That's what happened for Terri whose parents pollinated by identifying an opportune channel for her temperament and energy:

> When I was a child, I loved to run around with my siblings and go wild. I would take charge and lead the games we would play. I definitely had a loud mouth and knew how to use it. When I entered the fourth grade, my parents decided to have me join cheerleading. With my upbeat personality, tons of energy, and a domineering character with a loud voice, they knew that cheerleading would be just my sport. From that day on, I have cheered every year for eleven years. My parents saw that I loved to be the center of attention and loved performing and knew that cheerleading would fit me perfectly.

Terri notes that because she had such a passion for cheering, she learned skills quickly which built competence (and confidence) during those school years. She observes that rather than trying to tone her down (and conveying disapproval), her parents affirmed her and channeled her exuberance which she experienced as being treasured. The combination of her parents' treasuring, their attunement, and their creative pollinating helped Terri thrive.

Carla's mother was also attuned to her daughter's inclinations and sensitive to what they might mean. In Carla's case, the pollen was a flute:

> When I was little, my mom noticed I loved music and would sing along to jingles on radio commercials—and I'd always be singing the *instrumental*, not the lyrics. So she went out one night and bought me a secondhand flute, just to see if I'd be interested and learn the instrument. It turns out that I was and I loved it. I played all the time and joined the band at my school. I became the first chair flute at my high school and also auditioned and made it to the State Music Fair through middle school and high school. She noticed my natural interest in music and bought me my first instrument—which inspired me to play. I still love it to this day.

Clearly, Carla developed competence and her self-esteem grew stronger through the skill development and group social experiences that followed from her mother's pollinating love.

On a very different note, Mel had spent her first three years of college locked into a view of her future majoring in occupational therapy. The major had been difficult, and she was facing a do-or-die test in a key class. Her boyfriend was very aware of the extreme stress she was under and had been watching her wrestle with this major for quite some time:

> He began talking to me about the love for animals he'd seen in me and how happy it made me to be around them. He asked me if maybe I would rather work with animals than with people. He had noticed a potential within me that I had never really thought of. My love for animals is much stronger than my love for occupational therapy. I had never thought of that as an option, but agreed that working with animals would be more fun. With his simple question, I began thinking of changing my major and eventually did so. I couldn't be happier with my decision. Without my boyfriend's pollinating challenge love, I might have stayed stuck finishing a stressful major that would have eventually led to a job that I (probably) would have hated.

For Mel, the eyes of love saw something she hadn't seen for herself, and by giving her that insight, her boyfriend "helped me to put my feelings in order and determine what meant the most to me." His insightful questions and observations were central to her identity search, looking for a line of work that fit with her true self.

"Something I've noticed about you through the years is..."

Dan credits his older sister with pollinating love in his life. Her own life was in shambles after a near-fatal illness of her infant daughter and then the death of her young husband:

> I was there for her every day, as much as I could be, and I talked to her about everything. I just tried to help her through this rough time in her life. I still didn't know what I wanted to do when I got out of high school. Then one day my sister asked me to help her out with a particularly hard problem. She then told me she thought I should go to school to be a psychologist because I was really good with talking to people and soothing them. I hadn't been aware of this as a strength, but she recognized the potential in me and now I'm in college studying clinical psychology.

Potential is usually thought of in terms of specific gifts or talents, but it can also be thought of in terms of the kind of person we can become—our potential for character development. In the following example, Chad's grandfather sowed seeds about core values:

> When I was about fourteen years old, going into my freshman year of high school, my grandfather gave me a serious talk about the different paths and decisions which would unfold while I was in high school. He talked with me about how important it was for me to learn to make good decisions for myself, to be a leader and not a follower and to "be the bigger man." This conversation between my grandfather and me has stuck with me for a long time and always will. I took his advice seriously and to this day, I always operate on what is best for me, refusing to just go with the flow of a certain group. My grandfather is a very family-oriented man and is always looking out for everyone in the family. His decision to have that talk with me grew out of treasuring me.

Chad regarded this man-to-man talk as a form of mentoring that helped him develop a positive identity. He credited his grandfather with inspiring him to use his own autonomy for making choices rather than going along with his peer group if that might potentially spell trouble. He also felt strengthened to follow his own purpose of leading himself and others in positive directions. Chad was able to stay away from the bad kids in the school and make the decision to associate with the more stable kids who would help him perpetuate further positive development. "My grandfather's advice essentially inspired me to be the best I can be."

Pollen can also come in the form of affirmation that causes us to take ourselves seriously and believe in ourselves. In the example below, the affirmation and encouragement from Suzie's uncle crystallized her belief in her abilities, turning an idle pastime into a pursuit that became important to her emerging sense of self:

When I was growing up, my brothers always used to play baseball and I played right along with them, never thinking it would go beyond backyard fun. We were outside playing one time and my cousin's dad came up and said, "Suzie, you're really good at playing baseball." I looked at him curiously and said, "Really?" I took what he said into consideration and signed up for the town baseball team. Pretty soon people in town were telling me that I was awesome at it, which encouraged me to play softball in junior high, high school, and my freshman year at college. As just one of the crowd in the neighborhood, I had never thought I was any good at baseball, but after my uncle's compliment, I felt a sense of purpose about playing the game. Having him tell me I was good at it gave me the motivation and ambition to do it really well. It made me willing to risk trying in a bigger way.

In summary, pollinating adds a missing ingredient. Sometimes it plants a seed. At other times, it adds the light that helps a person see what's already there. On still other occasions, it draws together multiple factors in a way that helps self-understanding crystallize. The common factor is that attentiveness and attunement on the part of the love-giver enables them to offer the needed gift.

11

Challenge Love Confronts Differences Respectfully and Carefully

So far we've looked at acts of love that communicate messages boiling down to "I think you're great! Go for it! Keep it up! How can I help?" But we all know that things aren't always that easy. Different people see things differently. They want different things, need different things, interpret things differently, value things differently, prioritize differently, etc. You get the idea. There's conflict in even the best relationships.

I'm turning now to the most difficult action in love's repertoire, the act of disagreeing without damaging the relationship. It's as hierarchical as a parent disagreeing with how a child behaves and disciplining them (discipline means *teach*) and as egalitarian as equal friends or spouses having to negotiate the different things they want for themselves, for each other, and from each other. As I've said, there are plenty of books about parenting and my focus is on confronting respectfully in adult love relationships.

Although most people have a negative reaction to the word *confront*, it simply means to meet or to come up against, and we come up against differences between ourselves and those we love continually. It's inherent in being separate persons, and once we've emerged from that cozy *dual-oneness cocoon* described by Mahler, we tend to more openly vie for our own agenda.

All too often it's about what we want *from* the loved one instead of what we want *for* them. This is a very important distinction I first encountered in Sherod and Phyllis Millers' presentation of the Awareness Wheel (see note 10 for chapter 5). In any issue involving another person, to fully understand the *wants*, we have to break them down into three types:

- Things I want purely for myself that will gratify me.
- Things I know you want for yourself and which I also want for you. Sometimes your loved one wants things for themselves you don't want for them. For example, my child might give me a Christmas wish list that includes several computer games I don't want them to be playing. Or my spouse might want a piece of sports equipment that will tempt them to go away even more weekends when I already wish for more time together. There may also be things I want for you that you don't want for yourself. For instance, a parent might want their child to have a chance to go to college, but the child may have no such aspiration.
- Things I want for our relationship with each other.

When the Gottmans conducted follow-up interviews with couples over several years, the ones whose marriages were deteriorating revealed a common theme: one or the other or both saw the other person as having become selfish. Individuals who had once taken each other's wants and needs into account and even made sacrifices for the loved one had allowed self-centeredness to reassert itself and become a habit.

An observation I made earlier is important enough to repeat: the appearance of selflessless during courtship is largely deceiving, even to the one being apparently selfless. Yes, if we're honest about it, the degree of generosity and self-renunciation when we're *in love* surprises even us! Admittedly, in some cases it's calculated and even manipulative at times, but most of the time it takes place unconsciously and at least for a while, it's effortless. If the person involved in the romance could tell you what's actually going on as it happens over time, you'd hear something like this:

> I'm hopelessly in love with you, so *my* happiness is completely dependent on *you* choosing to be with me. Consequently I'm more than willing to sacrifice all sorts of personal wants and even needs because they seem unimportant to me right now in comparison with my overriding priority of getting you to want to be with me. (You get married or move in together. Time passes, addictive brain chemicals subside, the navigations of day-to-day life settle into a routine, and now...) Hmmmm... well I have a lot of wants and needs that have been part of my personality and way of life for a long time. I'm pretty tired of putting them on hold to make sure you like me. It's my turn now.

As I explained in chapter 3, it's inevitable that individualities will reassert themselves as two people emerge from the cocoon. But self-centeredness doesn't have to ruin love. In fact, making a commitment to learn how to really love each other can be a powerful motivator to grow out of that immature me-first tendency that tempts all of us to varying degrees throughout our lives. The problem is that learning a constructive way of dealing with differences takes self-restraint and determination, and, most of all, a genuine desire to develop habits that consistently honor both people. The best time to develop these habits is early, during the practicing phase of separating from the enmeshment, long before the ambivalence about how the attachment restricts your freedom has taken hold and fueled either person's sense of entitlement. (You might want to review chapter 3 on ambivalence.) Habits of mutual respect and being careful to understand each other's wants and needs will serve any relationship well over the long haul.

Carol J. Sherman, PhD

We'll look at three kinds of situations we all encounter in relationships in which being able to confront differences in a respectful and careful manner is perhaps the most important hallmark of real love. The first involves two people needing to make a decision that affects both of them and each wants different things. It can be as mundane as which kind of pizza to order or as far-reaching as whether to accept a job offer or to have a child. The two individuals may simply want things that are mutually exclusive, but it's often more complex than that. Often, each person has multiple competing (even conflicting) desires within themselves.

It's helpful to sort out the difference between *wanting* and *needing*, a distinction people often use to manipulate discussions of this kind. If you build a fairly simple habit into your relationship, you can minimize this kind of manipulation of each other. Before either of you claims to *need* something, be prepared to answer the question: "Of what will you be deprived or what debilitating thing will happen if you don't get it?" If the anticipated consequence is minor, it's probably a *want* rather than a real *need*. This step doesn't solve every dispute, but it often helps put things in perspective.

The second kind of situation involves times when your loved one is pursuing something you see as ill-advised, and it doesn't directly involve you. In these situations, it's hard to critique someone and recommend or ask for change without being experienced as controlling and rejecting. If you want to love well, it's important to learn how to do it carefully and respectfully.

The third kind of situation involves your loved one behaving in ways that are undermining your relationship with each other. Their decisions and actions are eroding your ability to believe you matter to them. Mutuality is disappearing and will continue to fade away unless a slide towards self-centered behavior is reversed or misperceptions are corrected. Many people I have counseled ignore the obvious fact that if you value the relationship, you don't let other priorities cause you to neglect it or press you into treating it carelessly.

Think of the relationship as a one-of-a-kind glass sculpture you both love dearly and can hold in your hands. When you address a conflict with each other, each of you has responsibility to protect that sculpture from words and actions that could chip, crack, or break it. Being in a hurry when talking about a tension-filled issue almost inevitably puts the sculpture at risk, tempting you to just fling it on the table or toss it to your loved one as either of you rushes out the door. When we're annoyed and feeling pressed for time or feeling put-upon, we're often reckless in the words we say to each other. Metaphorically, we crack and break off parts of the sculpture when we do so.

Sometimes you know ahead of time you're going to be dealing with tension around your different wants or needs. At other times, a shared decision you thought was going to be a snap turns out to open Pandora's box. Either way, love takes care of the relationship by creating time—now or later—where the two of you can give it your careful, respectful focused attention. Doing so says "we're not going to be careless with the trust we've built between us—the shared trust that we matter to each other." This shared ongoing commitment to mutual respect and mutual regard is what keeps a relationship strong.

Situation One:

We Have a Joint Decision to Make and Our Wants Don't Match Up

It helps a great deal to form a mutuality habit to fall back on when these situations come up and Appendix B (Puzzle It Out) can help you with that. It's important for each of you to know all the factors contributing to your own and each other's various agenda where a particular decision is involved. We can get very emotional and dismissive with each other unless we've committed to respectfully understanding each other's perspective.

Often, a decision is no big deal, and gathering extensive background information is overkill. That happens when your wants line up with each other's easily, either because they happen to be the same or because one of you doesn't particularly care about the outcome. In these cases, there's no need to find out all the pieces to a puzzle.

However, we all know that life in relationship is often not that simple. You want different things, and one or both of you are very invested in having your way. It gets even more complicated when one or both are dealing with multiple competing wants just within yourself. For instance, Jake and Missie have four different options for where to be at midnight on New Year's Eve: a party at Jake's best friend Bill's house, a party at Missie's brother Ted's house, a downtown pub where several friends are gathering, or home together. How should they decide? Each of them has yeses and nos connected with each option for various reasons. Missie wants a less-noisy setting than the pub, but she likes the people gathering there. She wants Jake to be happy and she likes Bill, but he gets to see Bill all the time and she wants to see her brother, but she doesn't like how Ted's wife acts at parties when she drinks too much. Jake wants to hang out at Bill's; he loves the pub scene usually, but not this particular pub; he likes Ted. Sometimes both of them are just in the mood to skip parties altogether, but that might not be the case this New Year's. Only if they have a commitment to really check in with each other about how each experiences the pros and cons of each option—so that each person is fully taken into account—is the importance of their relationship with each other honored. Quickly made decisions that make one person feel cheated may not be a big deal if they happen only occasionally, but if they happen often, it can erode trust.

When your wants differ from the wants of someone you love, it's important to take time to understand what's at stake for them in the decision, what makes it matter to them. It may be minor or, as the Gottman's discovered, there may be a "life dream" connected to it that gives it far more meaning than you realize. Sometimes the person with the life dream at stake doesn't even realize that's what's making this particular issue so charged for them. If it means a lot to one of you and the other person doesn't bother to understand the issue better, the sense of mutuality suffers. The erosion can be subtle at first, but when a couple doesn't protect their relationship by developing the habit of puzzling it out to really know each other well, hurts accumulate and selfishness takes hold.

My own approach to puzzling out issues can be found in Appendix B. Mutuality takes time and energy. Couples need to be prepared for the reality that once their natural separation from the cocoon starts to happen, they must forever after be intentional about their devotion to each other.

You can use the practicing stage of the attachment-separation cycle to safeguard your relationship. While there's still plenty of good will between you, practice bringing up problems via softened startup (a Gottman term) and puzzle them out between you. Essentially, softened start-up means making sure your tone of voice, facial expressions, and body language are friendly, rather than attacking. With that in place, you bring up the issue with some form of "I'm concerned about X's effects on you" or "I'm having a problem with…" and describe what makes the situation problematic for you. If you practice softened startup while the in-love chemicals are in your favor and you still have a sense of humor toward each other, you'll have a better chance of doing it well when tensions arise later on. See Appendix C for more on how to introduce problematic issues more effectively.

When people have left the cocoon and routines have set in, they tend to get careless with the very breakable sculpture they created together. Softened startup and puzzling things out take time, but when you don't address issues early, it's too easy for the negative side of that predictable rapprochement ambivalence to gain strength and add to the erosion of the attitude essential to love.

Situation Two:

Giving Feedback That Recommends a Change

Every person reading this book can tell stories of times when they've thought someone they love has been going down the wrong road or has been undermining their own well-being, either knowingly or blindly. When someone matters to you and, from your point of view, they are straying off course, you want to help them get back on track. You want them to see themselves as you see them and benefit from your perspective—and so you tell them what you see, hoping they'll wake up and make some changes.

"I'd like you to take the time to hear me out. Here's what I see when I look at you and your situation."

This is among the trickiest of all the behaviors of love. The examples from my clients and students will give you an understanding of the types of situations I have in mind, even though the approaches they report aren't always respectful or effective. It is hard to do well, but there are tools in the Appendices that can help you learn the skills.

When a recognized hierarchy exists, we expect critique even though we may not like it. For instance, an employer has a right to evaluate an employee and ask for change; a teacher has the responsibility to correct errors; and parents have responsibility for disciplining their children. But when two people regard themselves as equals, asking for or suggesting change is a different story.

Unfortunately, most of us approach it in a controlling, heated, or argumentative way—a style the Millers call *control talk*.[2] Abrupt in-your-face criticism generally triggers defensiveness, self-justification, and a counterattack, escalating into argument. And it rarely stays on topic, so it doesn't bring the self-reflection that was the original goal. Either we do it poorly or we avoid the topic altogether and walk away, simply leaving the person to continue wearing their blinders or we may even walk away from the relationship altogether. Because we're so inept or avoidant, we often prompt a fight, hurt the other's feelings, or leave them mystified about why we disappeared from the relationship.

Before I go further, let me be clear that not all confronting is *love* in action. Quite the contrary, much confrontation is anger, resentment, hatred, impulsiveness, selfishness, fear, and the like. I'm not giving you license to be confrontational in these negative ways. But respectfully and carefully presenting a loved one with data and your thought process, and asking them to consider it is another matter. Learning how to do it well—and learning how to receive it when it is so offered—is central to how genuine treasuring coupled with careful confrontation can help us mature.

Let's face it, we all do make mistakes, lose our perspective, lose sight of our goals, etc. at various times. All of us are farsighted, at least some of the time, and we need the constructive criticism of people who treasure us—trustworthy people who can see the bigger picture and help us sort things out. Even so, when we're in one of those blind spots or caught up in those details, having someone hold up a Caution sign, Reduce Speed Ahead, or a Stop sign tends to make us prickly if not downright put out:

Jo was complaining to Meg about her husband expecting her to drop everything she was doing when he was given the second half of a Saturday off unexpectedly. Meg chose her words carefully as she pointed out that only a couple of weeks before, Jo had been unhappy that Ted wouldn't set aside his work on his beloved motorcycle to join her on a spur-of-the-moment outing. It was a hard pill for Jo to swallow, this evidence that she wanted the freedom to rearrange his plans when it suited her, but didn't want to grant him the freedom to rearrange hers. The atmosphere got a little chilly between the friends, but the next day, Jo thanked Meg for helping her see a hard truth about herself. Because Jo knew that Meg treasured her, she was able to accept the sting, and after metabolizing it, she knew that Meg was helping her see a dynamic that had been hurting her marriage.

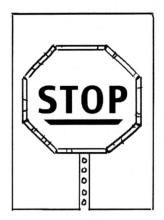

Confronting as an act of love is subject to misuse and abuse because unfortunately, we're all prone to pursue our own self-serving agenda in the disguise of "what I'm telling you is for your own good because I care about you." Because we all know this about ourselves, we feel justified in warding off, discounting, or ignoring input and feedback from others.

If there is a hidden self-serving agenda in the critique, the person being confronted and asked to change will nearly always see and resist it. Therefore, part of the hard work in carrying out this love action well is honestly examining your own motives beforehand. You don't have to refrain from critique just because you have mixed motives. Especially if you're being harmed by your loved one's actions, you do have a stake in the outcome. You just need to have the integrity to own up to the mixed motives if you want to retain your loved one's trust and willingness to listen:

> Bill's son, Eric, was looking for a job. Bill knew Eric had wanted for a long time to be a paramedic and when Eric started looking at openings with the local ambulance service, Bill outlined all the possible drawbacks he foresaw if Eric tried to go to school while working there. Eric had been aware for a long time that his dad's dream was for him to work at the family business with his uncle. Because Eric was so aware of this agenda, he didn't seriously consider the points his father made about combining school with the ambulance job.

Most situations that prompt us to confront a loved one in this way fall into one of two categories:

(1) As you see it, your loved one is behaving inappropriately or engaging in behaviors that are damaging to themselves. Parents disciplining their children obviously falls into this category. This helps account for why, forever after, when someone takes issue with your actions, you may want to fire back with "You're not my mother/father so stop telling me what I can and cannot do!" Using softened startup helps reduce the likelihood of triggering this kind of instantaneous defensiveness and counterattack.

Confronting love shown by extended family often makes a big difference in our lives. In the next two examples, a grandfather and then an aunt are able to get the attention of teenagers making poor choices:

> I have a cousin who struggled with alcoholism. His alcohol problems affected his work, schooling, and relationships with his family and friends including myself.

> Our grandfather is extremely involved in our lives, and my cousin was closest to him growing up because he was the firstborn grandchild. My grandfather is the one who confronted my cousin. His worst fear was that my cousin was going to get defensive and retreat but because he respects my grandfather so much, he did the opposite. My grandfather simply told him that because of the alcohol, he saw his grandson in a way that he had never seen him before, and that his actions were hurting his entire family who love him so much. He told him that the alcohol was blocking him from all of the dreams that he has longed to achieve and that if he did not stop, he was undermining his own well-being. If he did not change, he would suffer and my grandfather did not want to see that happen to him. Grandpa was being honest with my cousin, and after this confrontation, my cousin really stood back and took a look at how the alcohol had negatively affected him. Hearing feedback from a man he admired so much made him realize he needed to strive for the values that his family has instilled in him, and to strive to spend his time doing what gives him hope and a sense of purpose instead. Getting rid of the alcohol, he was able to start applying himself to the goals he had originally chosen before taking this road.

Another student, Cammy, wrote about confrontive and tough love she received from her aunt:

> My Aunt Betty Ann has always been the person giving me confrontive and tough love in my life. I've run into trouble my fair share of times. In my teen years, I knew that when it came to being yelled at for doing something wrong, I had more to worry about from Aunt Betty Ann than from my own mother. I have to say I never really appreciated her tongue lashings until I got older. When I was young, I thought I hated her for always telling me how it really was. I got mixed up with a bad crowd in my junior year in high school. I knew when my aunt heard

about the trouble I'd gotten into, I was done for. She wasn't actually as angry as I expected, but her disappointment in me was really troubling. She explained to me what the long-term consequences of my actions would be and how my life would likely turn out if I let my actions continue to be shaped by the crowd I was spending time with. At the time, I didn't understand and was very angry that she insisted I not hang out with those so-called friends. Looking back, I appreciate that she confronted me about my choices and told me the truth. My identity was headed in a bad direction through the company I was keeping. My aunt showed her love by redirecting me to healthier choices.

Trish shared her story of respectfully confronting an eleven-year-old girl she cared about whose posts on social media were troubling:

> Her foul language, making fun of people, and putting herself down worried me. I was concerned she was going to end up in trouble for cyberbullying and also create a bad image for herself due to the pictures she was posting, so I spoke to her about it. I let her know that I loved her very much and told her that she's a very smart and pretty young lady. I told her she needed to be careful about how she presented herself, especially on the Internet. I let her know how her mean words can affect the people she's saying them about. She was upset at first, but mostly because she thought I was mad at her. I told her I wasn't mad, just worried that she wasn't embracing and being the wonderful little girl she really was. Thankfully, she did take my advice and listened to what I said. She stopped the bullying and inappropriate posts. I think it built her trust to know there were people who loved her and were looking out for her best interests.

Friends sometimes wonder if it's their place to interfere in the choices being made by people they care about. There are many times when the attempt to hold up a mirror in this way backfires, even if done carefully and respectfully. Nevertheless, when someone matters to you enough, you may choose to take the risk. Bonnie's story is to the point:

> When I was in high school, I had a major problem with smoking pot. I stopped taking classes seriously and my grades dropped. I also stopped exercising and became lazy with my chores, my homework, and stopped hanging out with my close friends. Eventually, it affected my softball performance and I was benched for a couple of games. After this happened, my friend Sarah who has known me all my life sat me down and confronted me about my problem. She said she missed her old friend and how I used to be. She stated the facts about my laziness and my lack of dedication to the softball team. After she confronted me, I felt terrible about myself and ashamed for how I had been acting. I am thankful she sat me down and told me how it was.

(2) The second type of situation that calls for confronting your loved one for their own good is when they seem blind to how a romantic relationship is undermining them. It's not big news that people in love tend to be blind and the theme of good friends in bad relationships is a common one for students in my classes:

> One of my cousins was dating a guy who did not treat her right and was not in the relationship because he loved her, but because she was better off than he was. She was very blind to this, thought she was in love, and couldn't see that he was no-good for her. He was bringing her down and ruining her chances of success, making her quit a good job because, according to him, she wasn't home enough. I had to explain all this to her because she's always listened to me and understands where I'm coming from. I ended

up staying with her for a couple of weeks and pointing things out to her that she wouldn't have seen if I hadn't been there. After a lot of explaining, she finally understood she could do better than him and couldn't figure out why she was with him in the first place. It took a lot for me to talk to her about this, but I did it because I love her and could see how far she could go in life without him holding her back.

Situation Three:

Asking for Change Because Your Relationship is in Jeopardy

The third situation involves respectfully confronting someone you care about and asking for change because their behaviors are undermining the relationship itself. The Nurture Love and/or Challenge Love actions that once demonstrated that you mattered to them have begun to disappear, leading you to question their love for you. You wonder things like "Do they still think about my needs when they make decisions? Is their love for me diminishing? Am I still in their heart at all, or are they just going through the motions?"

If the differing wants concern how you're treating each other, things become a lot more complicated, far beyond what I can address here. The Gottmans found that although sometimes relationships come apart due to huge breaches of trust like affairs or misuse of family funds, more often there's a gradual erosion that begins with turning away and turning against a partner's bids for connection, followed by not bothering to repair "regrettable incidents" and essentially leaving the negative feelings to fester. As this happens, negative thoughts and feelings towards the partner become what Gottman calls an absorbing state. Picture a juice glass of clear water into which many, many drops of blue food coloring (representing selfishness) are added. Now add a few drops of yellow (representing considerateness or generosity). The yellow disappears, absorbed by the darker blue. In other words, once you've concluded your partner's selfish, mean, lazy, etc., you become more likely to dismiss something positive they do as a fluke. In your mind, the bad absorbs and cancels out the good.

Many times, we just let a relationship end. It's not worth it to us to work through the problem, whatever it is, and we either walk away abruptly or just let it fade away from neglect. At other times, we lash out in frustration at how the other person's behavior affects us. Emma shared a situation that's all too common:

> I had a good friend with whom I'd partnered in a lot of sports. He's extremely competitive in all things athletic and in one gym class competition, we came to the finals and I missed two plays at the end so we lost. He was a terribly bad sport about it. The next day, I told him off in no uncertain terms about how his competitiveness is excessive and I described the negative impact it has on a lot of his relationships. It was hard to hear, but he's grateful I "let him have it."

It's pretty clear Emma confronted her friend in what the Millers call a fight-talk manner, which is how it often happens. Some relationships can weather that kind of telling off and some can't. Learning how to confront straightforwardly and in a respectful manner is generally a preferable approach!

Jim's relationship with his parents had always been difficult, and he had never felt treasured. Their careers had always seemed more important and he was pretty bitter about it. As a young adult, he was tempted to write them off altogether, but his girlfriend hoped something more might be possible and encouraged him to talk with them. As a result of her encouragement:

> I spoke with my mom over winter break about the manner in which she parents us, about how it's not allowing her kids to grow into confident adults. My mom and I had an open discussion for almost an hour and I got my point across. She didn't say a lot at that time, but the way she's acted since then makes me believe she thought more later about what I said. That was the first time in my life I had ever done anything like that and her response made me feel I could do it again even though she didn't enjoy it. This has deepened my trust, allowing my mother and me to have a more intimate relationship now that I have brought us together. I will be more able to initiate another conversation about family matters instead of abstaining and feeling guilty about having issues we need to talk about.

It's become clear to me through the years that all of us are more likely to let someone's hard-to-hear critique get past our defenses and have some influence if we honestly believe that person genuinely cares about us, that we *matter* to them. The critique still may draw blood, but it will be the blade of a surgeon and not an attacker. "The wounds of a friend can be trusted," as an old saying goes.

In summary, only when the loved one feels treasured—that is, truly believes it's the well-being of their own true self that matters to you—only then is confronting really effective in fostering genuine positive change. Of all the actions of love, this one—confronting in a respectful manner for truly loving reasons—is by far the most difficult one to do well. It's the one we do poorly most often because we're tired, running short on time, or because we lack complete information about what's going on. It's the one where our own ability to be honest with ourselves is most important because if we don't recognize and eliminate or at least acknowledge our selfish motives, the loved one will see them and ignore any real validity in what we've said. It's the one most likely to prompt the other person to leave us, even when we do everything possible to do it well. So it's risky. But when the timing and the manner of delivery are done well, "speaking the truth in love" is one of the most important gifts one person can give another who matters to them.

The following lengthy example from a student will bridge us to the fifth action in the Challenge Love category, that of taking a stand when respectfully confronting a loved one with feedback hasn't brought about the reevaluation and changes you hoped for. In this case, Becca's mother tried to respect her growing autonomy as a young adult free to choose her own relationships and confronted her fairly gently with her concerns. When her daughter's health was obviously deteriorating, this mom took a stand:

> I began dating a boy who was much different from me and different from anyone I had ever dated. Soon my mother began noticing changes in me. I was oblivious to what was happening and kept insisting nothing was wrong. She tried to get me to step back and evaluate my relationship with him, pointing out how he was using me and how his negative treatment affected my moods. She wanted me to try and see my relationship from her perspective because she didn't want to see me get hurt. I kept denying everything she was observing, turning a blind eye to what was actually happening. My mother confronted me out of love to attempt to save me early on from this extremely negative relationship, but being a new college student

chasing after independence, I ignored what she said. The relationship got increasingly worse over the next few months as I changed into an almost completely different person. Not only did he lie to me about parties and drug involvement, but he made a comment about thinking I was overweight which affected me deeply. For the next few months, I ate only a granola bar or a few crackers every other day. My weight decreased rapidly, my hair began falling out, dark circles appeared under my eyes, and I was cold and tired all the time. My mother came to visit me at school and as I met her to let her into my dorm, she burst into tears. She had not seen me in a couple of months and was shocked by my appearance. She was so heartbroken that I was letting a boy get to me like this. She gave me some *tough love* and took a stand at this point which I needed badly. She told me that if I did not end things with this boy, she would not help me pay for college. She told me that if I didn't start eating again, I would wind up in the hospital; she wanted to support me, but was not going to watch me become sick. She was so worried that she threatened to take away the most important thing for me—without her help, there was no way I would be able to attend college.

It took her saying that she would not help support me anymore to make me realize I was making horrible decisions. I was choosing an unhealthy, negative relationship with a boy I had known for just a few months, a boy who didn't really care about me at all, over the amazing, lifelong relationship I had with my mother (who had *my* best interests at heart).

My mother's tough love helped me realize what an unhealthy relationship looks like, so that if I should ever find myself in one again, I know I need to leave as soon as possible. The whole situation, including the confronting and tough love, helped strengthen several ego strengths in me. My mother's actions helped my basic trust in her deepen even more as I realized she doesn't point things out to intrude but for the purpose of protecting me and teaching me. I learned more about myself and my identity—that I don't want to be a sickly thin girl who can barely function, but a strong healthy girl who doesn't let the opinion of a rude boyfriend control her. I also learned there are still certain situations in which I am not ready to be completely autonomous yet. I still need my mother to help me see things I may not notice, especially when it comes to relationships because I do have a tendency to be kind of oblivious.

With Becca's lengthy example, we'll turn now to taking a stand, the action the recovery movement has called tough love.

12

Challenge Love Takes a Firm Stand Against a Loved One's Destructive Actions

True discipline exists only within a hierarchical relationship and the best discipline teaches. A person in authority over someone else first articulates the behavior they're looking for. If the person of lower rank does not comply, the superior will generally point out the lapse and ask for change. If that change isn't forthcoming, there will either be a reward system to create incentive for the desired behavior or a punishment system to deter the negative behavior. Even within established hierarchies, one of the best ways of pursuing change is to respectfully confront the other person and help them consider the possible, probable, or certain consequences of their actions.

But what are your options when you see destructive tendencies in someone with whom you are an equal and that person matters greatly to you—a friend, spouse, sibling, or even a parent, once you become an adult? You want them to change, to stop harming themselves—and others, which may include you. If you have already tried confronting them carefully and respectfully with the evidence of how their actions are harmful and that hasn't been effective, your devotion to their well-being (as well as your own) may require you to resort to an ultimatum. You may have to take a firm stand, saying "No more. I love you too much to in any way help you continue what you're doing because it's so destructive."

As I said above, the concept of discipline is inherently hierarchical. It assumes the person confronting has authority over the one being confronted. So long as I am dependent on you in some way, it is your power (or my fear that you will exercise your power) that forces me to change my behavior. But as a child grows, both in size and in mental ability, for a parent's discipline to effectively help the child mature as well as simply survive, that parent must begin helping the child-teen understand how the changes being promoted will contribute to the well-being of their own true self. Parents who insist on obedience purely as submission to their authority are not doing much to help their child become ready for taking on adult responsibilities.

The essence of loving an adolescent well is gradually letting go the reins by which you have been guiding them, gradually relinquishing the hierarchical relationship. It can be nerve-wracking and often is. And as the adolescent becomes more and more independent (a process that's drawn out for many by financial dependency in the college years), the power of a parent changes to merely having input and perhaps influence on their offspring's ways of thinking about life, decisions, etc. The transition from parental rule to self-rule is often a very difficult one.

Barbara told of a situation in her teen years when her grandmother was keeping her and her little sister while her parents were away:

> My grandmother didn't really know the rules and although I didn't have my license yet, I asked to go pick up a friend with the car. When my grandmother said "okay," we went for a joyride. My little sister blackmailed me so I told my parents. They let me go ahead and take my driver's test three weeks later, but once I had passed, they confiscated it for three months as punishment for what I'd done. I was

really angry, but in the future every time I was put in a bad situation, I thought back to that punishment and made a good decision in place of a bad one.

Ron described his father's sustaining love as pretty comprehensive well into his late adolescence, doing everything he could to provide for his son's needs. Unfortunately, Ron dug himself into a very deep hole, spending thousands of dollars on drugs and jeopardizing his credit. His father had been down that road himself and in an effort to get through to his son, he took a firm stand:

> My mother was being ultra-supportive of my efforts at recovery, but my father reached the point where he had had enough of my crap. I needed a reality check and my father gave it to me. His use of tough love did push me to become a more productive than destructive person. I was actually quite surprised at how fast I could change my act once my father took away all the perks I had been enjoying for so long. Having that stint where his supportive love was almost gone helped motivate me to fix the problems as soon as possible.

My client Trisha's experience, as summarized below, is from the point of view of a parent. When Trisha's son began high school, he started acting out and back-talking his parents. Throughout his freshman year, she and her husband tolerated the behavior with only minor efforts to curb it. After a very public screaming match on the front lawn, they put their foot down. They took away his cell phone and put an end to watching television and having friends over. He was also required to come home directly after school—all of this until his attitude improved. In addition, he was not allowed to play basketball his sophomore year. He saw these restrictions as very harsh, but consistent enforcement for about two months brought about a significant change in his behaviors. He began helping around the house, did his homework, and complied with the requirements. Trisha reported a lasting improvement in their relationship.

And here is my student Carly's memory of being on the receiving side of that kind of tough love:

> I met a new friend, Tara, the summer before entering eighth grade. She was experienced in a lot of things I'd never thought twice about doing, but I was thirteen that summer and thought I was queen bee. At first, my new behaviors were only small changes, things like walking around town late at night, wearing a lot of makeup, and changing how I dressed to be more like her. Then I stopped hanging out with my old friends (since she didn't like them) and hanging out with her friends instead. Then she introduced me to drugs, cigarettes, and alcohol; and I didn't see any problem with it. My cousins were also involved and when their mom told my mom, she was extremely upset. That's when I got a taste of tough love. She grounded me for the rest of the summer. I could only have friends over if my mom was home and couldn't see Tara at all. My mom bought me *Go Ask Alice*, a book about teenage addiction, and threatened to send me to an adolescent rehab center. She stopped giving me an allowance and instead put it in a savings account. I had to apologize to the old friends I'd stopped talking to. There were strict rules about visiting even the one friend I could still go see and it felt like being under house arrest. I was really mad at my mom and thought she was being mean and unreasonable. I yelled at her and told her she was ruining my life and I know that was hard for her. Looking back, I couldn't be more grateful. Really, she was trying the best way she knew how to help me. Her tough love saved me from going down a terrible road and creating a bad future for myself.

Within my framework, this kind of tough love means that you show your ongoing treasuring of the person by withholding some or all of the sustaining actions and many of the facilitating forms of Challenge Love you have been providing. A person reaches this painful decision and carries it out with difficulty only when their best efforts at challenging the loved one to see the truth and change have not worked:

> Barbara's twenty-six-year-old son, Carl, had used her naïve love for him to get money for the OxyContin to which he was addicted. She had tried for years to talk him out of using, trying to convince him that he was skilled enough to make a good living at computer programming and that he was attractive enough to find a good wife. Carl continued to live in her basement, work at odd jobs, and occasionally sell things he thought she wouldn't notice or make a fuss about. Finally, Barbara realized this could go on forever if she didn't make a change. In spite of her fear that he would fall even further into trouble, she told him he had to move out and she changed the locks on the doors to prevent further theft. She told him she loved him and would support any real steps he took toward recovery.

Peg described how her friend's efforts to confront her fell on deaf ears until finally Peg was left to deal with her bad situation on her own:

> I was constantly being mistreated by my boyfriend and always felt awful about myself as a result. My in loveness blinded me from the truth. I would call my best friend, crying, and she would always try to mend the broken pieces he had caused. Eventually, she was fed up with my crying phone calls and told me she just wanted me to be happy again. She said that what my boyfriend was doing was called abuse and that I needed to take care of myself by leaving the relationship. I was in denial at this point and assured her that it would get better. I did not easily accept her confrontive Challenge Love…and that resulted in her taking a stand. It came one day when I called her crying yet again about a fight with my boyfriend. She said that enough was enough. There was nothing else she could do or say to make my relationship better and told me that if I

> was going to continue to date him, then she was no longer going to talk with me. I remember being so angry with her. We had been best friends for over ten years. How could she put me in a position where I had to choose between her and the man I was "in love" with? Foolishly, I made the wrong choice. I stayed with my boyfriend and my best friend stuck to her word and discontinued talking with me. Sure enough, he hurt me again but this time I had no friend to talk to, to help me through it. She was the person I had always called…and now she wasn't answering my calls. She had disappeared from my life. It was really hard getting used to. Eventually, I began to realize that everything she had told me from the start was true. It took me a while, but I broke up with him and my friendship with her began once again where it had left off—except this time there were no crying phone calls.

Peg realized that the confrontive and tough take-a-firm-stand love didn't feel treasuring at all at the time. Far from it. It wasn't until these actions had played their part in helping her change her situation that she could recognize the love that had motivated them. In the end, she saw her friend's love as a manifestation of the intimate friendship they had built over time and a manifestation of care. In the long run, her friend's actions contributed to a deepened trust in the friendship.

Hank described another fairly common situation between friends at college. His roommate had changed from a weekend party drinker to someone who drank almost every day:

> My other roommates and I finally took action and gave him some tough love. We took some of his possessions like his iPod, cell phone, and his Xbox until he agreed to seek some help. He threw a huge fit and was yelling at all of us. He said that he was going to call the cops if we didn't return all his stuff right away. We tried to explain to him that we were doing it because we cared about him, and we didn't want him to drink anymore. After about two hours

of him going back and forth fighting with us, he finally went to the guidance counselor at school. He agreed to it just to get us off his back. After two weeks of sessions with the guidance counselor he completely changed. His drinking problems went away. He took my two other roommates and me out to dinner soon after that to thank us for helping him out. He knew at that point that we had been tough on him because we all cared about him. He still drinks once in a while but he isn't the dumb drunk he used to be.

Sometimes the threat of withholding is sufficient. At other times, the actual withdrawal of support has to take place. Taking a firm stand within marriage is hard to do, but is sometimes absolutely essential:

This type of love has been given by my aunt to my uncle due to his drinking. She had warned him in the past that if he didn't stop drinking, she was going to move back to her home state with their children. Over the course of a few years, he continued to drink and made no change to his behaviors. In order for him to realize that what he was doing was destructive to the family and to himself, she left. She loves him and wanted to keep their relationship going, but realized that unless he changed, none of them would be okay. My aunt loves my uncle and therefore never came out and said "you're an alcoholic," but rather said, "I'm concerned for your health and your relationship with your children and me." She was not judging him for having a bad character, but was insisting that his behavior was unacceptable and that he had to make a choice. After my aunt left, my uncle realized he needed to stop drinking. He recognized his behaviors as degrading and dangerous. He was able to repair and rebuild his relationship with his wife.

Sometimes taking a stand with a loved one brings about a life-giving result. At other times, taking a stand even in the most loving way possible doesn't work and the self-defeating or self-destructive behaviors continue. Even when feeling hopeless about the chances of success, love makes the effort:

> Confronting someone you love can be one of the hardest things to do, especially if they are close family. My Aunt Becky has a lot of drug and alcohol addictions, and ever since my grandmother died, her addiction has just grown rapidly. My family has tried to confront her about her issues, and she always tells us how she is going to get better. We finally got her to go to rehab, and we thought that all of the talks that we had with her finally worked. When she got out she was better for a few weeks, but went right back into her addiction. My family didn't know what else to do but to tell her that they were going to cut off their relationships with her until she could really make the effort to get better. My whole family has tried to help her as best we can, but she has to want to get better and she doesn't. My family and I are ready to help her the minute she is willing to get rid of her addiction.

Students often tell of occasions when the roles have been reversed—when it's been an older child or teenager who has done their best to confront a parent in trouble. In the account that follows, Buddy made the first move, but it wasn't until his grandfather intervened that enough was at stake in his father's life to bring about the change:

> Although my childhood with my father had a lot of great times, there were also some darker days for us. When I was eleven years old, my father experienced a serious head trauma from a physical altercation. He was in the hospital for almost eight months and he was blessed to make it through. This unfortunately led to an addiction to prescription pain medication as time went on. This was something that had a dramatic impact on both his life and mine, and there was a point where I had to confront him. I was thirteen years old when I decided to confront my

father about his addiction with pain medication. This took a lot of time and courage to think of how I was going to address the issue, but I made sure to let him know that it was for his own benefit, not only mine. I told my father that he needed to change, and that these pain pills were making him into a different person. It hurt my father to hear that what he had been doing was hurting me as well, but we both left the conversation not knowing if my words would be enough to make him stop. My father continued to struggle with his addiction for about a year after I confronted him on the issue. It was finally to the point where someone needed to take a stand and bring his addiction to a stop. My grandfather forced my father to go to rehab or else he would lose custody of me. This was a very difficult time in my life because I knew my father might not be able to overcome his addiction. Luckily today he is living as a healthy drug-free individual, and our bond is still very strong.

Taking a well-thought-out stand against a loved one's destructive behavior is an extremely difficult form of love to carry out. It "just doesn't *feel right*" to withhold Nurture Love and supportive Challenge Love, so it is very difficult to hold firm to one's resolve while treasuring tugs at the heart and pleads for leniency. One should only take a stand like this if they have thought it out carefully enough to truly believe it is absolutely necessary. Only then can they commit their willpower to see it through.

Concluding Comments

Love is a way of life. If we're fortunate, we learn what that way of life looks, feels, and acts like by receiving it and by watching the people around us love each other well. Ideally, those same people also help us practice taking others into account appropriately, and we begin to experience the joy that comes with living our own life this way. By receiving love, seeing love around us, and being helped to practice loving behaviors, we are guided into this way of life.

For the many who did not have good guides early in life or who have become confused by mixed messages along the way, I have offered some of the clues I have found most helpful. To begin with, I helped you see that the *feeling* we call love is only the entryway to the fullness of what love really is. I linked that emotion with treasuring the other person as somehow part of your very sense of self, as having a place for them in your heart and feeling tenderness toward them as a result. I explained that when someone is experienced as part of you, their safety is one of your highest priorities in life and you take their well-being into account in all the choices you make. It's hard to be consistent in this attitude that relativizes your own wants and needs, but the effort to do so is a central hallmark of love. I also told you that if you genuinely love someone and value their well-being, your actions will actually contribute to building them up.

Another of the clues I gave you is that it isn't easy. I unmasked the ambivalence we so often experience about attachment, wanting the benefits a committed love relationship provides while simultaneously wanting the benefits of freedom. I pointed out that there is self-centeredness at the core of every one of us and that love requires us to take others into account as mattering just as much as we matter. A conscious choice to try and love well always bumps up against the me-first starting point of human nature. A readiness to apologize for the times when selfishness, thoughtlessness, carelessness, or laziness win out is a key part of the journey. So is accepting your loved one's sincere apologies when the shoe is on the other foot.

I provided you with Erik Erikson's clues, insights into character strengths to help you see that if someone matters to you, you want them to be resilient, able to handle the hard knocks of life, and able to pursue their interests and develop their unique gifts. I described the ego strengths that help a person begin crystallizing personal values and a sense of selfhood as they move toward adulthood.

I shared clues from John Gottman's work, insights into the skills of attunement so that readers can start noticing and responding to their loved ones' bids for nurture and support in ways that build greater trust.

And finally, I described and gave real life examples of the behaviors that nurture and challenge us into resilience. You can now see the simple yet powerful ways our actions can convey "you matter to me," fostering the development of ego strengths in the people we love, whatever their ages.

I hope these new lenses will help you see what you need to see so that your own life and the lives of those around you can be enriched.

Appendices

Appendix A: Erikson's Developmental Stages
Appendix B: Puzzle It Out
Appendix C: Confronting Issues Respectfully
Appendix D: Self-soothing Techniques.

Appendix A

A Really Short Version of Erikson's Stage Theory

Here is an outline of how *in the best of all possible worlds*, key people love a child into having the tools needed to be relatively well-equipped for life and relationships.

- Trust and Hope: Reasonably dependable, reliable, kind-hearted nurture allows a child to feel secure, to trust that needs will be met, and to experience hope about life and faith, first in people and eventually, perhaps, in some greater transcendent power. [When care is inconsistent or provided without a good attachment, the outcome is relative insecurity, mistrust and hopelessness.]

- Autonomy and Willpower: Encouragement of the older infant's assertiveness within the bounds of safety, of course, fosters the beginnings of autonomy/independence and enthusiasm for applying himself or herself to a goal which at first is as simple as getting across the room to a toy or reaching the cup on the table or eating one food instead of the other. This is the earliest manifestation of willpower and it can be either encouraged or stifled. If the child is already trusting and hope-filled, they are more likely to assert their will in ways the caregivers can appropriately affirm. (When caregivers are excessively controlling or stifling of the child's freedom to be assertive, the outcome is relative self-doubt.)

- Initiative and the pursuit of Purpose: In the midst of wanting to assert autonomy, the toddler gradually becomes more and more aware that they are quite a separate individual from the nurturer and because that relationship is the source of everything he/she needs for physical and emotional survival, this realization prompts a vague concern about whether it's okay to venture forth. If encouraged to pursue the things that interest them, to try out new options, to risk stretching the limits as they feel inclined to do so, the child's confidence is likely to grow as will the belief that they can freely come and go from the nurturer as their base camp as they pursue whatever goals arise. (When a person is pursuing a goal, they have a sense of purpose). (If the caregiver openly or subtly conveys they are wounded by the child's increasing ability and desire to strike out on their own, the child will feel guilty about becoming a separate "individuated" person with wants of their own apart from the caregiver.)

- Industry (Diligence) and Competencies: Strictly speaking, the ability to grasp an object with their hand is a competency, so infants are engaged in this quest quite early. The older toddler, however, becomes very intent on learning to do new things that signify "I'm getting to be big and strong and able to do things!" Hope, willpower, inner freedom to pursue purposes—all of these add momentum and encouragement to the quest for mastering new skills and knowledge sets. As the child's body and brain continue to mature, the accumulation of cognitive, physical, and social competencies pours supplies into the inner container, however you picture it, where a sense of self-worth rises and falls in response to how the person thinks about the emerging and functioning self. (Mistrust, self-doubt, and guilt in any degree and combination hold a child back in the pursuit and acquisition of competencies in various arenas of life. Consequently, they are likely to actually *be* inferior on certain measures and/or to evaluate themselves as inferior. Whether based on objective performance measures or on misperception based on self-doubt and guilt, such negative self-evaluations put holes in the bottom of what I have called the inner self-worth tank.)

Each ego strength becomes a resource that increases a person's likelihood of engaging life's next/other challenges well. Life challenges you to use the resources and by doing so, they become more and more a part of who you are as a person. When life knocks you down, it can deal a blow to any of the tools (i.e., when someone betrays your trust; when exercise of independence gets you in trouble; when pursuing an interest, dream, or idea costs you relationship with someone who just couldn't "go there" with you; when an effort to accomplish something ends up in failure). When these experiences come along in life, it can be really hard on the sense of self-worth, even if the trust or willpower, etc. were off to pretty good starts. If they were shaky to begin with, setbacks can make you feel even more like the rug's been pulled out from under you. Those are the times you need concrete evidence that you are treasured anyway by the key people in your life. That's when sustenance from others helping you over the rough spot can really strengthen your trust in humanity. That's when love in the form of support, sometimes teaching or coaching, or even constructive criticism, can help you learn from your mistakes.

- Identity and Loyalty/Faithfulness: Hopefully, as an adolescent begins to fully engage questions about the values that will guide them and the goals worth pursuing, they have accumulated enough of the already-named resources to work with. The self's need to begin resolving these larger questions takes on greater urgency as launching from home approaches. If the true self has been encouraged and supported all along, it will move into this quest with a good supply of resources for the tasks ahead. By late adolescence, some true selves already know "what they want to do with their lives" and others don't. The Nurture Loves and Challenge Loves are uniquely needed in a person's decade-long (sometimes lifelong) process of deciding who to be, what to stand for, and how they want to affect the world around them—their identity, formed around self-chosen values to which they want to be loyal or faithful. (Confusion about these things can persist even if the person is listening to their true self, but the confusion is likely to be stronger and persist longer if they lack the ego strengths or began to form a false [accommodating] self earlier in life.)

- Intimacy and Mutuality: As a young adult moves toward launching from home and becoming their own separate center of gravity for life, the desire for trustworthy companionship on the journey is the deepest longing of their true self. If their true self has been nurtured and supported all along and they have a good-enough supply of the ego strengths, they are well-prepared to develop intimate relationships—to risk opening up and being known emotionally, intellectually, socially, physically, spiritually, and psychologically; and to make room for knowing another person or persons in those ways. Developing companionships at this level helps a person explore their true self further and consolidate their identity. When a connection grows at this deep level of knowing and being known (intimacy), the other person's well-being matters to you as much as your own, Erikson's definition of mutual love or mutuality. (A person's capacity for intimacy and ability to love in this fully mutual way is greatly affected by how much basic trust/hope/faith is at their core and the degree to which they experience themselves as operating out of a true, authentic self. If their core is porous or they feel inauthentic because they began long ago to operate out of a false self, they are likely to remain largely hidden from their peers. Such a person may prefer a lifestyle without much social interaction, but even if they are apparently sociably engaged in the world and even if they get into a committed pair-bonding relationship, their true self will experience isolation and loneliness. Literature and life are filled with examples of people who are *saved* by the love of another person who sees or senses their true self and "tames" them by providing the Nurture Love and Challenge Love that were missing earlier in life.)

- Generativity and Care: Technically, adolescents on the other side of puberty can generate new life, but Erikson used the word *generative* to characterize adulthood with its focus on creating a family and/or being productive in the world of work. The ability to care for others by nurturing and raising a family is a key part of generativity, but it is much more inclusive of the ways adults contribute positively to the world around them. In terms of my own framework, the best care manifests an ability to attune to others and respond willingly with Nurture Love and Challenge Love appropriate to their needs. (Those who lack the ability because of missing ego strengths or lack the willingness because of excessive preoccupation with the self are likely to experience what Erikson calls stagnation—their lives produce little of value.)

- Integrity and Wisdom: At some point in the aging process, an adult begins to slow down in their participation in generativy and care for the world around them. Sometimes, this is linked with formal retirement from a job or career. At other times, it may be prompted by an illness, injury, or general deterioration of health. Whatever the timing, some version of a retrospective review of life begins to take place, and inevitably, there is an assessment dimension to it. If the person has lived consistently with consciously chosen values, for the most part, the mix of fulfillment and regret will likely yield a sense of integrity and there's a good chance they will be regarded as a source of wisdom about life. (People whose true selves have remained in hiding and unfulfilled, or whose relative lack of ego strengths have compromised their ability to succeed on the things they regard as important are likely to experience at least moderate despair and sadness as they come to the end.)

As I have already explained, it is utterly misleading to look at Erikson's stage theory in the stair-step chart form so typical of psychology textbooks, as in the example below. Even though he is the one who presented us with that kind of visual presentation of his work, it perpetuates the beginning psychology student's naïve misunderstandings about resource development being over and done and then you move on.

It is more helpful and accurate to visualize the accumulation of ego strengths using a modification of the baseball diagram, clearly showing where the resilience comes from. Picture each core ingredient permeating the outer layers to the extent each was added as the ball was forming. Then, whatever is in your baseball, that's the ball you take with you into the game of life. You take that into the opportunities to form intimate relationships, make a new family, and participate in the world around you. By no means is this a perfect image either, since the depth of layers is misleading, and you can't see how each resource permeates the other ones. But if you could imagine each ego strength inside the ball emanating an energy uniquely its own that radiates to and through the other layers, you'd get the idea.

You Matter to Me

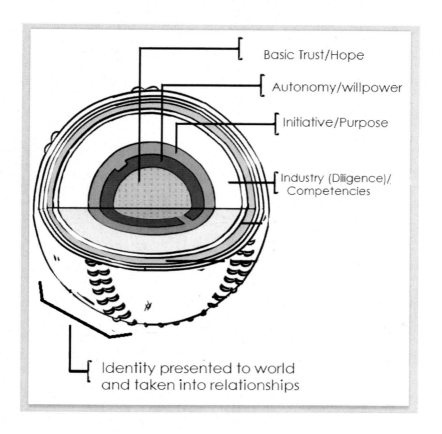

Appendix B

Puzzle It Out
A way to communicate better

Whether it's couples coming in for help or individuals lamenting past or current relationship problems, "we just don't know how to communicate" is a refrain counselors of all types hear over and over again. Self-help authors are continually creating and re-creating approaches to help people deal with their differences when problematic issues arise. All of these authors share a common goal of helping their readers respectfully present their point of view and respectfully receive the viewpoint of their relationship partner.

As I've explained in Part II, mature love between adults is characterized by what Erik Erikson calls "mutuality." By this he means that the other person's well-being matters to you just as much as your own and you behave accordingly. There are three major underminers of mutuality where communication is concerned: biology, misplaced priorities where time is concerned, and entitlement. These enemies of love are sneaky and it's important to understand them so you can defeat them. "Forewarned is forearmed."

Carol J. Sherman, PhD

Underminer of Mutuality:
The biology of Fight/Flight/Freeze (Fold or Collapse)

It's that key word "respectfully" that's so hard to accomplish since at the very first hint that we're not getting something we want, it seems to be human nature to automatically shift into self-protective and/or competitive mode. We even go on the attack. Actually, it's not human nature so much as it is our animal nature. Realizing that fact and counteracting it is more than half the battle toward communicating better.

In biological terms, when fulfillment of a moderate or strong desire seems in jeopardy our brain and body go from one part of our nervous system --the part that facilitates social engagement -- to another more primitive part whose sole agenda is survival (see note 6 for chapter 5 on the work of Stephen Porges). Animals don't respect each other. Through instinct and experience they may come to recognize another's superior cunning or strength and bow to it, but that's not respect in the human sense. Encarta Dictionary says respect involves thoughtfulness, consideration and "deferential admiration". Deferential means being polite, courteous, even submissive. So to respect another person with whom you have an issue means to remain polite while you submit to hearing each other's point of view so both of you can take both of you into consideration appropriately. The trouble is that if you've gone down the "DANGER!" neurological pathway, this stance of openness to influence is already badly compromised. When the primitive brain's fight/flight/freeze (fold or collapse) program takes over, our "thinking brain" is used in service to the goal of defeating, escaping from, or pacifying the person perceived as a threat, not cooperating with them.

My point is that any perceived threat to getting what you desire automatically triggers "Issue! React!" just as instinctively as the dog, Doug, in the movie "UP" freezes, points, and shouts "SQUIRREL!". Our animal nature hijacks our higher potential as human beings and once we shift from an all-is-well mode into that "protect and defend" mode things go downhill fast in the communication department. The defensive reaction can be to argue (fight), to leave the conversation altogether without engaging (flight), or to abandon one's self and just accommodate the other person without making any effort to be taken into account (freeze/collapse/submit). These biological reflex actions don't build or sustain trust.

The only solution I know of is to try and put a circuit breaker at the brain's junction box between the two neurological options—the social engagement and the fight/flight/freeze paths. **The only way to accomplish *that* is to firmly establish ahead of time that you are both physically and emotionally safe in this relationship.** If you haven't been safe in previous family or couple relationships because the other person *hasn't* been committed to your well-being, this new belief will be hard to come by. But it's absolutely central to your hope of being able to communicate with each other instead of automatically protecting yourself by arguing, withdrawing, or submitting.

I'm going to repeat that because it's the cornerstone of everything else I'm going to say here. If two people want to learn to communicate effectively with each other, ground rules that establish the physical and emotional safety of both people have to be in place at the start and both of you have to be committed to them. As Sherod and Phyllis Miller explain in their excellent communication materials available from Interpersonal Communication Programs, Inc., both people (i.e. everyone involved) have to start from an "I count; you count" premise. That's the essence of Erikson's definition of mutuality and the central affirmation of my definition of love: you matter to me. And if you matter to me, I want first of all to protect you *even from myself* and second, to fully understand the issue from your point of view. Only then can I take you into account appropriately.

Carol J. Sherman, PhD

Establishing this ground rule promise to rein yourself in and force yourself to go into "curious and exploring mode" rather than "attack and defend mode" is absolutely essential. And anytime either of you notices your own blood pressure reaching the red zone or senses the other is tipping over into the danger zone (relationship gurus John and Julie Gottman call it flooding), you simply HAVE TO take time out to get your physiology back into the social engagement system. THAT's the only way empathy, understanding, and creative problem solving take place.

Sometimes in the midst of a heated communication session one person's intense desire to resolve the issue may make it difficult to allow the other person to step away from the engagement. This may be especially true if that person has made a habit of just walking out on difficult discussions in the past, never returning to resolve the issue. The Gottmans recommend agreeing to a ten minute time-out during which time the flooded party or parties focus attention on something else entirely such as a crossword puzzle or reading an amusing magazine article. This refocusing of attention is an important part of cooling down one's physiological arousal. One of the safety ground rules should be that both people will respect either person's call for a time out. Another ground rule is the promise to return to the discussion after the time out.

It really is that cut and dried. The problem is that most of us don't want to do it. We're not motivated enough to restrain our inner Dobermans and rely on our inner Golden Retrievers.

So how do you establish that kind of confidence that you're safe? Only through consistent, repeated experiences of respectfully hearing each other out and taking each other into account. That's the devotion strand of the three-stranded braid that makes up genuine love, explained in chapter One. You make it a rule of life between the two of you that mutuality is going to prevail in your relationship and then you develop habits of explaining yourself thoroughly and listening to each other attentively, habits that make it a reality. You both commit to paying attention to the Matter Meter, explained in chapter 4, making sure you never act like you can take your partner or leave them—that is, like they no longer matter. Slipping back into self-centeredness is human nature, but you make a decision to not let yourself go down that road. You make mutuality such a fundamental shared value that each of you has permission to send up a signal flag if selfishness rears its ugly head or the Doberman starts bearing its teeth or growling. That signal "flag" could be saying "I'm sensing that you (or I) just shifted into fight mode (or flight mode or give up mode). I'd like us to take a breather."

If maintaining mutual love is the deepest desire of both hearts, you'll be motivated to learn the skills for taking each other into account and you'll exercise the necessary self-discipline required for communicating effectively: both the speaking and the listening parts. As you accumulate experiences of taking each other into account appropriately, your trust in this particular relationship will grow and you'll become more able to rein in the impulse to defend yourself or go on the counter-attack.

Underminer of Mutuality: Shortage of Time

Shortage of time—or at least perceived shortage of time—seems to be one of the most dangerous enemies of mutuality. If you want the other person to understand where you're coming from, you need to be able to lay the issue out on the table clearly and thoroughly--so they can learn how you see it. Before you can do that, you have to sort yourself out and understand the factors shaping your reactions and desires where a particular issue is concerned. If you've sorted yourself out pretty well ahead of time using the technique below, it probably won't take a lot of the other person's time to hear you out. Sometimes all we truly want is to be respectfully heard and, hopefully, understood. If you develop a true partnership of mutuality, you may even become each other's facilitators in figuring yourselves out.

Of course if the issue is an interpersonal one, that is, if there's an issue between the two of you, more time will be needed for the other person to be heard on the issue, as well. Only then can you allow mutual influence to take place rather than mere turf protection. We don't create or devote that kind of time unless we really do believe that taking both of us into account is the only way to love well, the only way to protect a relationship we treasure. As the authors of *A General Theory of Love* state, "relationships live on time." (See note 2 for chapter 6.)

The implications are unavoidable: any relationship deprived of time will begin to deteriorate.

Underminer of Mutuality:
Entitlement and/or The Repair of Earlier Wrongs

When you start identifying the puzzle parts in the desires category described below, you may very well come up against your own or the other person's hidden sense of being entitled to having a want or need fulfilled. In legal terms that means you act as if you have a right to it which creates a hierarchy over other people. That's the opposite of mutuality which assumes the wants and needs of both people have equal claim for being taken into account.

A sense of entitlement comes in many versions. Some of them are rooted in having had certain childhood needs met a little too well and being overly indulged. In these cases we believe we're "God's gift to the world" and therefore deserve special treatment. As a result we very naturally and complacently carry into adulthood our assumption of privileged status and continue to operate out of it.

Other versions are rooted in the exact opposite experiences, ie. being neglected or injured earlier in life. In these cases our unhealed wounded self lives on, secretly or not so secretly longing for safety and to have its needs finally met. Often in these cases we developed strategies for coping and protecting ourselves as best we could through pleasing and accommodating others; belittling ourselves or invalidating our own needs; taking it out on others weaker than ourselves; overly empathizing with others in an effort to form a connection; imitating other people's aggressive behaviors in the attempt to protect ourselves or get the reparation we think we deserve. Many of these strategies are implemented automatically later in life. We often act as if the current loved one did the harm and ought to make restitution.

When we have unresolved issues from our past, the ways of thinking, feeling and acting from that earlier situation function like little sub-personalities or parts of self. Think of them as "apps" on your smartphone created or downloaded (by watching others in real life or on various media) at earlier times in your life and never up-dated. It doesn't take much of a touch on the touchscreen to launch them. When we get hijacked by these wounded or protective "brain apps", we become blind and deaf to the requirements of mutual regard in the present. Although overly simplified, the movie *Inside Out* portrays it well: one part of you might be saying sadly "It's hopeless to think I'll ever matter" and another part is shouting angrily "Are you kidding?! It's MY TURN!!" And to the extent we do think about it, we feel justified in our actions. In a sense, however, we're thinking with the brain of the three year old or eight year old who created the original app. When we're in the grips of a hijacking brain app, we've lost touch with our most adult self's belief in and commitment to mutuality within this adult relationship.

The more arrogant form is fairly easy to recognize and expose because it's blatant. The "poor me" disguise is more insidious and hidden and is more difficult for others to address since having it named is usually experienced as wounding. It doesn't seem fair that so many of us reach adulthood burdened with one of the forms of entitlement, but it's a reality. Try and remain open to signs that you, too, may need to guard against this underminer of genuine mutual regard.

Substance Use...and Abuse

There's one last thing that needs to be said before we get to the "how to" of puzzling out an issue. Our ability to communicate respectfully and effectively is often undermined by consuming alcohol, marijuana or other substances for the sake of helping us relax and unwind. Many people turn to alcohol and drugs at a young age to dull or escape the pain of neglect or abuse. Others develop the habit while in high stress jobs from which they want to down-shift quickly—Emergency Medicine staff and surgeons, firefighters, high-stake investment professionals, business CEOs, members of the military, and others. Still others turn to mind and mood-altering substances out of boredom with life. Whatever the motivation, these folks often build up a high tolerance for their substance of choice and have a hard time recognizing the negative effects on their relationships.

If you're one of these individuals, it's important to realize that when under the influence—even if you "feel fine"-- you are far more likely to get hijacked by your brain's less-than-respectful apps. You're far less likely to be able to puzzle out your issues well or to effectively hear the other person's puzzle. While substances may temporarily dull whatever tension you seek to escape, your cognitive clarity and emotional self-control become dulled as well. That means you become less safe to communicate with, and please remember my earlier point that safety is essential for effective communication. Even if you do no visible harm, you're definitely far less likely to remember the conversation accurately and benefit from any empathy, insights, or resolves that emerged from it.

If you're feeling defensive right now just reading this section, it's a fairly good sign you have a reactive part of self (possibly from your teen years) rising up against being told what to do and what not to do. If your loved ones really do matter to you, you'll recognize your defensiveness as probable confirmation that you're in denial about your substance use and there's a problem. Please take that warning signal to heart. It's time to stop pretending your substance of choice is harmless since it's robbing your loved one of your best self and of the safety you promised them. Do whatever you have to do to break off the relationship with your substance so that you can love well the person to whom you've made commitments.

When Issues Arise...

In my experience of myself, my friends, and my clients, issues arise primarily when we don't get something we desire. Whether a desire is a true need or "just a want" is a matter of interpretation, of course, and, as I explained in chapter 11, a helpful way to distinguish between them is to ask "What bad thing do I believe will happen if this desire isn't fulfilled?" If the answer reveals something that clearly undermines your physical, emotional or spiritual well-being, it's probably reasonable to put it in the need category. Maybe not everyone would need it, but you do. If nothing particularly awful is likely should the desire go unmet, put it in the category of a want, i.e. optional. Of course we can all use this distinction to manipulate others if we choose to, but I'm going to give you the benefit of the doubt: You're striving toward true mutuality, neither over- nor under-inflating the importance of the desire involved in a particular situation.

The Issue Puzzle

There are many readily available images and methods for sorting out issues, including various wheels of awareness like those of the Millers (presented in *Connecting*) and Dr. Dan Siegel, promoter of mindfulness training. You can readily find information about these online. I offer clients and students the following technique of finding pieces of the inner puzzle and putting them together.

When you're feeling mixed up or irritated or overwhelmed by an issue, this is a way to make some sense of what's going on inside. It may be an issue that involves just you or it may involve other people. Picture the issue, whatever it is, as a jigsaw puzzle you're pouring out of your brain onto the table. There's no box with a picture on it to guide you. Some of the pieces are face up and others are face down. The ones that are face up are the factors you're already consciously aware of even though you may not yet understand how they relate to each other. For instance, you already know you're angry; no surprise about that! Or you already know what set you off was stepping in dog poop in the yard. Or maybe you already know you're agitated because you want to go to a party, but you have a big assignment due tomorrow. Those are helpful starting places. Go ahead and name them. Jot them down.

But a lot of times, we know we're anxious (piece facing up), but we aren't consciously aware yet of what's causing it (pieces facing down). Or we have to make a decision and don't know what matters to us most. Or we've learned a new piece of information and can't figure out what we want to do about it. The task is to turn over the pieces, discover what's on them and see how they fit together.

If you're like me, you look for the edge pieces first when you start a puzzle so you can put the frame together. When you start an issue puzzle, there are several types of pieces to look for:

- desires (wants or needs);
- data from your five senses, intuition, and facts;
- feelings; and
- thoughts of various sorts such as interpretations, expectations, beliefs, opinions, etc.

You can start anywhere, really, but it can be especially helpful to identify the point in time when the issue appeared. Pick up the remote control on the movie of your life and play it backwards until you can see the instant at which the issue showed itself. Whether in a big or small way there came a moment when you were unsettled. It's the moment at which you could and perhaps should have said "Houston, we have a problem." Maybe you did say it to yourself or even to someone else at the time. In their communication materials referenced above, the Millers call it the point you feel a "pinch", a physiological signal that something's wrong. Many people describe a sudden twist, tug or wrenching in their "gut" while others report a tightening of neck or shoulder muscles. You probably know your own most common physical signal very well.

Movie directors are masters at showing their audience the pinch. Often the soundtrack signals it the instant the character sees, hears, touches, smells, or tastes something that triggers a thought, feeling, desire, etc. It may be subtle or blatant, but the actor lets us know by behaviors, facial expressions, body language, tone of voice or spoken words that an internal event has taken place. Given this explanation, most of my clients can do a replay of a morning, day, week, or even longer period of time and identify the point at which an issue arose.

Even if you don't understand exactly what happened, you can identify the timeframe when something changed in your mood or mindset and that's a very useful piece of information. So to begin an issue puzzle look back and find the "pinch". That's the point to start watching your internal replay closely so you can identify puzzle pieces and get clues about the bigger picture.

What did you see, hear, smell, touch (feel via your skin), or taste just before the pinch? Those are puzzle pieces, too. Realize that you may have different data available to you than another person involved in the situation. If you share what you saw or heard, for instance, your reaction may make more sense to them.

Ask yourself what emotions shot through you or gradually emerged as the issue developed in your head--and in your body since emotions have physiological counterparts. Label as many puzzle pieces as you need for these emotion words, each with one separate emotion on it. (Most emotions are identifiable in one word; any time you say "I feel that xyz" you're actually identifying a thought. It's a widespread habit of speech that's very misleading. Push yourself to identify the one word emotion that particular thought activated.) Zero to ten, now strong was the emotion? Has that changed over time? Happy, sad, angry, afraid and disgusted are the core emotions and there are infinite nuances to each one. I've put a list of emotions at the end of this appendix and you can easily find more extensive lists online to help you broaden your awareness of emotional nuances. (Unfortunately, not all of those lists do a good job of distinguishing between emotions and thoughts.)

Now ask yourself what thoughts went through your mind. This will probably tell you where each of those emotions came from. Generally, we feel what we feel because we're thinking what we're thinking. This old saying isn't 100% accurate since the most primitive emotions like anger and fear arise from our most primitive survival brain and happen almost instantaneously, split-seconds before the more evolved thinking brain has time to do its thing. (Then, of course, we feed that initial primitive spark with thoughts.) But for our purposes here, it works to think of emotions as triggered and fueled by thoughts. So ask yourself what you thought when you experienced an issue show up on your internal landscape. How did you interpret the data? Did you assume anything? Did you expect something different? Did you form a judgment or evaluation? For instance, if I see the sink full of dishes and interpret that as meaning my daughter's been on the phone with her boyfriend all evening, I might feel irritated. If I see the very same thing, but remember my daughter got a phone call from her aunt who needed a babysitter at the last minute, I might feel no irritation at all. So for each emotion puzzle piece, figure out as many contributing thoughts as you can. If you chase down "thought" with a synonym finder you'll see that belief, opinion, idea, judgment, theory, assumption, interpretation, analysis, and many other types of thoughts can show up as puzzle pieces.

With some pieces joined together now, the picture is probably becoming clearer, but keep going. See if you can identify similar situations in your past with this person or other people that help explain your strong reaction to the current appearance of this issue. These memories would go in the thought category also. It's pretty common for us to overreact emotionally when something happens that awakens unfinished business from the past. I ask my clients "How old did you feel when that emotion shot through you?" Eight? Three? Fifteen? Twenty-two? "Who were you reacting to at that point in your life?" If you had especially difficult experiences earlier in life and didn't have much emotional support at the time, you probably have undigested emotions lying around inside your brain and body, waiting to be reactivated. These, too, are like those apps on your touchscreen I mentioned earlier. When an experience today is reminiscent of the old wound, the well-practiced way of handling it often takes over. Sometimes it's the "I'm wounded" app, but very often it's a set of reactive emotions, thoughts and actions by which you coped as best you could. If you experience anger, sadness, fear, shame or guilt out of proportion to the current situation, there's a good chance you've been hijacked by a younger part of yourself. A book called *Parts Work* by Tom Holmes is an excellent introduction to this way of thinking about ourselves.[1]

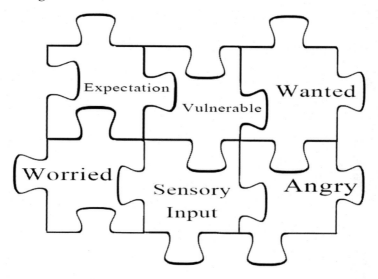

In the "thoughts" category, I find that expectations very often cause pinches. As Fred Luskin points out in his various works on forgiveness, a great many grievances arise from having unenforceable rules, set ideas about the way everyone ought to do life.²

It can be a small thing like "the right way" to cut carrots for Thanksgiving dinner or something much larger such as how long you're "supposed to" keep a car before buying a new one. Usually, we don't know someone had a rule or expectation until we've inadvertently broken it and "gotten in trouble," a phrase that already signals someone is in the parent role and the other person is in a child role—never a good sign when mutual regard is the goal. When this happens, a quick tool I've shared with clients is to answer the following questions:

- Exactly what was the rule that was broken?
- Who made the rule?
- What purpose did that rule serve?
- What person did that rule serve when it came into being?
- What positive thing(s) would be lost (by whom) if the rule were revised or dropped?
- What positive thing(s) might be gained (by whom) if the rule were revised or dropped?

Arguments can be often be defused by having a habit of non-defensively providing the answers to these questions when someone has tripped over an unspoken rule. The answers almost invariably show either the wisdom of the rule, its obsolescence and/or foolishness, or the self-interest hidden within it.

At any time as you're puzzling out an issue, insights and connections can come out of nowhere—as if puzzle pieces flip over of their own accord and show you how they fit into the picture. And it can help to have another person work on the puzzle with you since they can point out connections you may not be able to easily see. The more you trust the other person, the more open you'll be to benefiting from their possible insights.

As I've already mentioned, many issues appear because you didn't get something you desired or you got something you desired not to have. For these puzzle pieces identify: What did you want or need to happen instead of what happened? What did you want or need not to happen that did happen? What do you want or need to happen in the future that seems jeopardized by what has happened? When it's an interpersonal issue, the Gottmans advise giving the other person a "recipe" for how to make you happier. It's not that you're entitled to it, but it can be enormously helpful to articulate clearly what you'd like. Even the people who love us well and pay attention aren't mind readers and it's unfair and unhelpful to make them guess. In addition, requiring yourself to state it can help you realize you give mixed messages at times, possibly because you have conflicting wants within yourself, a situation that puts your loved one in a real bind.

The Gottmans also point out helpfully that some issues arise because whatever's happening has implications for larger life dreams that are competing or in conflict. This can be multiple desires competing within an individual—some of which are compatible with each other and some of which may be mutually exclusive-- or the competing dreams of two individuals in relationship with each other. Often the relational tension exists because neither person has yet articulated and dealt with their own multiple competing dreams! These are also very important pieces to the picture puzzle jumble that was in your head.

Whether you set out to just understand yourself better or to explain yourself to someone else, it's essential to see the desires, thoughts, feelings and data that make up the puzzle of you. Only then can you make an action plan that fits if one is needed.

When it comes to brainstorming possible action plans for yourself or for the two of you if it's a relational issue, I encourage my clients to think outside the box created by their past experience of themselves. To do this, pick five people you know (or even characters from history, public life, TV, film or novels) whose personalities and life experiences are very different from your own. Ask yourself what each of them might do in this situation and make a list of those options without pre-judging what comes to mind. After you've generated the list in this wide-open manner, consider those options from the standpoint of your value system and practical considerations. You may be surprised to discover some options open to you that you wouldn't have thought of otherwise.

Carol J. Sherman, PhD

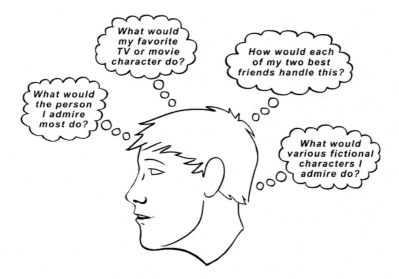

When the time comes for sharing your puzzle with another person, keep in mind that if there's any kind of power struggle going on in a relationship, both people tend to listen defensively. In any issue that arises, each automatically assumes the other is trying to gain control. It will build trust in the relationship to "show your hand" at the outset, that is, go ahead and reveal what it is you want up front so the other person isn't distracted by trying to figure out what you're leading up to, i.e. "the catch." For instance, you might say "I'd like 'such and such' to happen and here's how I'm thinking about it." Or "I'm leaning towards X where 'such and such' is concerned. I'd like to explain what's influencing me and hear the factors influencing you about it." Or you could say "I've been thinking about X and realize I have some strong feelings about it. I know you may have some strong feelings about it, too. I'd like to tell you where I'm coming from and hear what's influencing you. Either of us can go first." Then share what puzzling it out has shown you. (Once you establish safety and create these good communication habits with each other, you'll be able to drop some of the explanatory phrases that can seem pretty formal at first.)

Undoubtedly, puzzling out an issue in this way is time-consuming and it can be messy. You won't need to bother with it unless an issue is complicated or you're faced with a decision that is particularly important to you and you want to be thorough in thinking it through. If it helps you take yourself and/or a loved one into account in a more meaningful way, it's worth the time and effort.

Emotions

Many of us have a very limited awareness of emotions and may only be able to recognize that we (or others) are happy, sad, angry, afraid or disgusted—the big five, rooted in brain biology. (I've also met people who can't accurately recognize even these.) When a child isn't helped to regulate their emotions in the first year or two of life by an attuned and steady nurturer, they tend to just develop On/Off buttons in their brain to protect them from the overwhelming experience of "too much" of these core emotions. Relying on the Off button a lot, they don't learn to recognize the nuances of milder versions of the feeling in themselves or in other people. For instance, such a person will see little signs of irritation in another person and jump to the conclusion that the person is extremely angry since they didn't learn what the nuances look or feel like.

It's easy to find lists of emotion words online so my goal in providing this beginner's list is to give you a kind of gradient to help you identify for yourself and a loved one "where you are" on some emotions that tend to cause relational problems. Some might disagree with where I've put words on the gradients, but at least they'll give you a starting place as you work on your puzzles.

<u>Sadness</u>	<u>Disgust</u> (toward a person)
Unhappy	Dismissive
Gloomy	Disdainful
Discouraged	Belittling
Sad	Jaded
Depressed	Scornful
Lonely	Condescending
Demoralized	Contemptuous
Miserable	Utterly disgusted
Desolate	Filled w/ loathing
Devastated	
	<u>Disappointment</u>
<u>Confusion</u>	Hurt
Puzzled	Left out
Awkward	Wounded
Doubtful	Offended
Uncertain	Crushed
Mixed up	Heart-broken
At sea	Indignant
Mystified	Wronged
Unsure	Betrayed
Disoriented	
	<u>Anger</u>
<u>Embarrassment</u>	Irritated
Sheepish	Irked
Embarrassed	Annoyed
Unprepared (eval)	Cranky
Pathetic (eval)	Aggravated
Regretful	Angry
Worthless (eval)	Resentful
Ashamed	Vicious
Humiliated	Furious
	Enraged

<u>Fear</u> Uneasy Timid/hesitant On edge Hesitant Cautious Vigilant Afraid Alarmed Terrified Petrified <u>Anxiety</u> Uneasy Jittery Nervous Concerned Anxious Worried Troubled Tense Stressed Panicky <u>Surprise</u> Caught off guard Surprised Stunned Shocked	<u>Helplessness</u> (all are responses to evaluations which actually lead to feelings like fear or embarrassment) Vulnerable Unsafe Inferior Incompetent Inept <u>Impatience</u> Antsy Edgy Impatient Intolerant <u>Engagement</u> Bored Uninterested Curious Interested Eager <u>Weariness</u> (actually an energy state) Tired Fatigued Drained Used up Exhausted

Appendix C

Confronting Issues Respectfully

Much of the time, we raise issues in a manner the Millers call control talk in their discussion of styles of communication. The goal of someone using control talk is to make the other person do or stop doing, feel or stop feeling, think or stop thinking, or want or stop wanting. You get the idea. If the person speaking has authority over the recipient of the message, it may be appropriate for them to engage in this style, but hopefully they do it in a respectful manner. Sometimes in relationships between otherwise equal peers, one grants the other authority based on skill or a knowledge base. An example would be when my husband and I do remodeling projects together. He has a vast amount of experience and knowledge and so, by and large, I willingly let him use control talk to tell me what to do and how best to do it. If he tries that same style of communication in the kitchen where I have as much experience as he does, I'm likely to experience what the Millers call a *pinch* if he tells me what to do or how to do it.

People experience pinches when the pieces of their issue puzzle (see Appendix B) aren't fitting together smoothly: they perceive something with their senses (data) and interpret it (a thought), and if it doesn't fit with what they expected or wanted, they have a mild or major physiological reaction. Many people feel it in their stomachs, others in their necks or shoulders. You are probably very familiar with your own signal that you're not happy about what just happened.

Many relationship pinches happen when one person inappropriately tries to control the other, either through what the Millers call *fight talk* or *spite talk* (see Note 1 in chapter 11). And remember that "talk" includes body language, facial expressions, tone of voice and even silence. (Ignored bids can cause a world of hurt and anger.)

Fight talk directly tries to push or pull another person and often prompts blocking or dragging in the recipient. *Spite talk* indirectly tries to use power from a one-down position; perceiving oneself to be powerless, the intention is to thwart by noncompliance. In a sense, it's an attempt to control by refusing to be controlled.

Fight talk and spite talk are indications that mutuality is missing. The direct attempt to control inherent in fight talk does not take the other person into account appropriately, and the indirect attempt to thwart that's inherent in spite talk contains the message that "I don't feel taken into account appropriately."

The intentions behind fight talks are to force others into doing things, justify oneself and intimidate through behaviors like demanding, scolding, name-calling, and putting the other person down. Spite talk, on the other hand uses such tactics as sarcasm, pouting, procrastinating and whining to manipulate, trigger guilt, be pitied, and covertly fight back.

John Gottman found in his observational research on couples that he could predict divorce with an amazing degree of accuracy based simply on how they started up a fifteen-minute conversation about something about which they disagreed. He distinguishes between complaining—which is about a person's behavior—and criticizing—which attacks the person's character, often with *always* or *never* generalizations. In addition to criticizing, if contempt enters the room (some version of the message that "You're an inferior human being"), nothing good or useful is likely to come of the conversation. As you may have noticed, these are fight and spite talk messages and they cause major pinches in others.

If you know you are prone to contempt for others, love requires you to protect your loved ones from it. It's probably rooted in early rapprochement period wounds, so I suggest you reread chapter 3. Discounting or dismissing those who wounded you may have been a way of comforting and protecting yourself—and it grew into a very unfortunate preemptive habit. After all, if you regard others as inferior to you, you can justify discounting their importance. Sad to say, you probably have a significant dose of the arrogant type of narcissism in your makeup. Countless books have been written to help other people cope with you, but I haven't found any books to help you change your outlook. That's because relatively few narcissists recognize the need to change, so there's not much of a market for such a book. If you're the exception and you'd like help making some changes, you may find that reading some of those books might increase your empathy for those who live with you, and create enough humility to motivate you to change. I recommend *Children of the Self-Absorbed: A Grown-Up's Guide to Getting Over Narcissistic Parents* by Nina Brown and *Disarming the Narcissist: Surviving and Thriving with the Self-Absorbed* by Wendy T. Behary as good places to begin.

The Gottmans teach couples to start their conversation gently with softened startup, that is, with a complaint describing their own experience of the situation they'd like to see changed. Describe it nonjudgmentally and then ask for what you need or want, explaining what makes that desirable for you. Give the other person a recipe for what would work for you, says Gottman.

This approach pairs nicely with what the Millers call bringing up the issue using *straight talk* instead of fight or spite talk. To do this effectively, you take the time to puzzle out in your own mind what makes this an issue for you, including what you want and the factors that make you want it. In straight talk, you simply reveal the information from your puzzle, making sure you screen out any fight or spite talk. I tell my clients to imagine a walk-through screening arch like the security arches in airports. The fight/spite arch sounds an alarm if the words you are about to say, your tone of voice, your facial expression, or your body language are trying to directly or indirectly control the other person. To use the fight and spite talk detector to prevent yourself from causing a pinch, ask yourself "Would I speak to my boss or coworker this way and expect to keep my job?" (Would I use these words? This tone of voice? This facial expression? This body language?) If not, change to straight talk before proceeding.

Respectfully confronting a loved one in my framework requires you to first do the work of puzzling out the issue for yourself. If you're struggling to hold yourself back from criticizing or attacking, your brain has probably shifted your body into fight or flight mode, and your Militant Self or Bodyguard Self is now in the driver's seat. (For more on the idea of having a variety of parts of yourself, see Tom Holmes's *Parts Work: An Illustrated Guide to Your Inner Life.*) Your brain has *flooded* and in that condition, you're unable to listen well, think clearly, or remember you actually love and respect this other person. Try one or more of the self-soothing techniques in Appendix D to get your heart rate down and put your Devoted Treasuring Self back in charge. At that point, try and find some empathy for the other person by puzzling out the issue from their point of view as best you can. (See Appendix B.) This may help you find your way to a softer, gentler start-up. If, on the other hand, you feel intimidated and are afraid to raise the issue (you're in your Frightened Child Self), the process of thoroughly sorting out the data you're taking into account, what you think and want and the reasons behind those will help build your confidence to access your Adult Self and advocate for yourself.

After puzzling out the issue you want to address, remind yourself that you treasure this person and as you approach your loved one, express that treasuring directly in some way as part of raising it with softened startup. If you're using this book to help you get your relationship off to a good start, both of you will develop this habit during dating and courtship. If you get married, you'll continue it throughout "the honeymoon phase" and the "practicing phase" I described in chapter 3. It's true that over time when your partner begins a respectful confrontation with softened startup, you may start looking good naturedly for the punch line any time you receive a compliment, but that's okay. You can be pleasantly surprised each time no respectful confrontation follows! This ability to raise and discuss problems respectfully will become one of the greatest strengths of your relationship.

In conjunction with introducing the issue with softened startup, be sure to ask if your loved one has the energy, time, and willingness to discuss it or if you'd be more likely to have a more useful conversation at a later time and if that's the case, let your devotion to each other motivate you to agree on a time together. The Millers call this "contracting" and it only makes sense: if either of you is rushed, weary, not feeling well, or just in a bad

Carol J. Sherman, PhD

mood, it's not likely you'll be able to hear each other very well or empathize.

Use the guidelines in Appendix B for puzzling out an interpersonal issue to help you consider each other's viewpoints. The goal of mutuality is to take each other into account *in all things*. It's far easier said than done, but it is essential to loving well.

Appendix D

Self-soothing Techniques

The goal is simply to shift your attention away from whatever has triggered you so that your body can downshift out of the fight or flight response that has revved you up and is keeping you in a fighting mood. For whatever reasons, you are experiencing the other person as a danger, and your primitive physiological response has taken over your brain. You literally cannot think clearly, listen respectfully, or empathize when your nervous system is that aroused. You're like a car whose gas pedal is stuck and even pushing down. You are or soon will be out of control. You can train yourself to put on the brakes or at least take your foot off the gas pedal and let your vehicle slow down when that happens.

What's needed first is to acknowledge it happens to you. Next, recognize it's not okay to do that to your loved one. Third, take responsibility for not turning into the Incredible Hulk. When you stop feeding the fire, it will die down and turning your thoughts to something else is the most effective way to stop the flooding. There are many ways to do this. All that matters is finding a few that work for you. Here are some suggestions of things that work for other people:

- Listen to a few songs with lyrics that you like and which have the effect of taking you to a different place internally. (Make yourself a playlist for this kind of downshifting so you can get to it easily). Eventually, you'll be able to sing them to yourself in your mind anywhere you are, on any occasion, and bring about the desired result.
- Do a crossword puzzle or Sudoku.
- Shift your attention to your breathing and intentionally slow it down by "Inhale 2–3–4, hold 2–3–4, exhale–2–3–4–5–6–7. Remain focused and counting for several minutes.
- Inhaling adds oxygen and accelerates your body and brain whereas exhaling lets it coast and slow down. You can accomplish the same breathing change more enjoyably by singing or whistling out loud (even very softly). Doing so requires to you inhale quickly and then pace your exhalation to sing or whistle a long phrase.
- Distract yourself by picking up a newspaper, magazine or book and counting the number of times a particular letter appears on the page. Continue until your physiology has settled down.
- Go to a favorite relaxing place in your mind's eye—a lakeshore, mountain hike, ocean beach, your grandmother's kitchen, or a cabin in the woods. Tell yourself the sensory details of that place as if you're helping a friend picture it: what are all the things you can see, hear, touch/feel, smell, and taste. Some people think of this technique as changing channels on their inner television set.
- If you have a dog or cat, sit down and pet them for at least five minutes while reading something neutral out loud to them. Petting them is likely to release soothing oxytocin in your brain, but if you leave your mind free, it may just

get caught up in whatever triggered you in the first place. So pet them while reading out loud something that puts your mind on something else. Even if you're not with your pet, you can spend time with them in your mind, focusing on the sensory details like the feel of their fur and the sound of purring, and it may help you feel calmer.

Glossary of Terms

Many of these words are used in very specific ways by the psychologists who have influenced me. This glossary provides a quick reference for the relatively simple way I'm using the terms in this book.

ambivalence—Experiencing 'no' and 'yes' at the same time about something or someone.
anxiety—An underlying and pervasive sense of not being safe. A person may or may not know what is contributing to this uneasiness.
attunement—(1) Noticing another person's body language, facial expressions, silence, tone of voice, pace of speaking and other blatant or subtle clues that give information about what's going on in their inner world, (2) learning what those clues mean, and (3) responding with empathy.
autonomy—Ability to exercise control over one's own self in keeping with one's own will; independence. (Erikson)
bids—Verbal and non-verbal, direct and indirect, requests for some kind of response from another person. (Gottman)
care—Extending oneself to provide for another person's needs, enhance their well-being, or enrich their life. (Erikson)
Challenge Love—Actions that help another person develop the potentials of their true self by facilitating growth, accessing resources or overcoming obstacles.

cherish—To act in ways that clearly and directly demonstrate to another person that they have a place in your heart "right now". These actions are especially meaningful and effective in moments when you are actually feeling tender-hearted towards that person. For the most part, cherishing actions and thin Plexiglas (see below) go together.

coach (teach)—Use your own knowledge and skills to actively help another person develop them.

cogwheeling—Erikson's term for the fact that the stages of one person's life interact with those of other people in different or the same stages. Like gears meshing together and causing wheels to turn, one person's need to develop certain inner resources hopefully activates the ego strengths in people around them and each contributes positively to the other. This often happens intergenerationally, but it can also happen between peers.

compassion—A feeling of kinship, often temporary, that can arise when we see someone else's need. This sense of being connected can prompt Nurture Love or Challenge Love actions toward someone not previously experienced as part of one's self.

competence—The mastery of a skill or a body of knowledge. (Erikson)

confront respectfully—Bring up an issue with someone in which you think, feel, perceive or desire differently from them and do it in a manner that communicates they are important to you and matter just as much as you or anyone else.

control talk—Written, verbal or non-verbal communication in which the "speaker" intends to bring about compliance with what they want. (Millers)

counter-dependence—Active efforts to not need someone else. This is often a self-protective over-reaction to having been shamed for needing appropriate help during the early years.

diligence—(in place of Erikson's "industry")—Working towards a goal with persistence.

encourage—Convey to another person that you believe in them and their ability to endure or succeed.

enduring vulnerability—UCLA psychologist Tom Bradbury's term (popularized by Gottman) for the sensitivities a person brings to adulthood from difficult childhood experiences.

explicit memory system—One of two systems by which the brain encodes experiences via neurological pathways. This storytelling type of memory depends on the hippocampus and begins encoding experiences around age 3 in most children. The episodes we consciously remember tend to be ones that were repeated often or ones where there was a particularly strong emotional charge, either positive or negative, to set them apart from the mundane.

faith—(See hope)

false self—The idea that a child sometimes learns to excessively stifle their autonomy and initiative in order to gain acceptance, feel loved, or avoid punishment. When this happens, the child learns to become an actor and show the world a façade that accommodates others.

fidelity—The ability to stick to values one has thought through and chosen as one's own. It includes the ability to stand by another person who shares your values and to whom you've made a commitment. (Erikson)

fight talk—Body language, tone of voice, facial expression or words which directly and aggressively tries to be in charge and often conveys "there's something wrong with you". (Millers, Gottman)

flooding—When an experience arouses a person physiologically to the point where blood pressure, heart rate and stress chemicals are so elevated that they can no longer think straight. The ability to listen, concentrate, solve problems creatively, and empathize diminish and even disappear. (Gottman)

generativity—Adding another human being to the world through procreation or adding products or services to the world through the use of one's time, energy, and talents. (Erikson)

hatching—Mahler's term for the phase of child development (around the age of five months) when a baby's brain has matured to the point where they begin to actively process and organize the data coming to them through their five senses. A new degree of alertness is evident in the baby. I use the term to also refer to puberty as an emergence from childhood's relative cocoon, as well as to the emergence of starry-eyed lovers out of their romantic cocoon.

hope—Positive anticipation about the future. It is the product of experiencing other people as trustworthy and the environment as predominantly safe and supportive. (Erikson)

identity (self)—Children naturally and automatically take in and take on certain characteristics of the people who raise them. In addition they consciously model themselves after certain people as they grow up. Thus, the interpersonal environment as well as the physical hardships or opportunities of life circumstances greatly affect how the raw material of a person's genetic make-up takes shape. In adolescence and beyond, the person uses whatever ego resources they have accumulated to sort out how to interact on their own, apart from family, in their society/culture. In various writings, Erikson describes the sense of identity as a sense of well-being, of having sorted out for yourself the values you want to live by, of having a direction and a sense of purpose, of feeling at home with yourself. It's not as much about what you do for a living as it is about what kind of person you are. On the one hand, it is a lifelong "work in progress". On the other hand, it seems to me that most older people looking back on life can recognize that a "core" sense of self solidified some time in their twenties or thirties. "Mid-life crises" in identity sometimes come about in people who had a largely false self in early life (see above).

implicit memory system—One of two systems by which the brain encodes experience via neurological patterns of cells firing. The brain has the ability to learn (remember) patterns without our conscious awareness it is doing so and without our understanding of how it happens. Implicit memory begins functioning during an infant's gestation in utero and is not dependent on the hippocampus so central later to forming retrievable episodic memories. The implicit memory system holds much emotional memory and body memory without narratives to accompany them.

individuation—(See separation-individuation)

industry—(See diligence)

initiative—Pursuit of interests and goals that express one's individuality as a person separate and different from one's attachment figures. (Note: This is decidedly different from the way Erikson talks about the third stage and its ego strength.)

integrity—When a person approaches the end of life, whether it is in old age or illness brings life to a premature end, they reflect on the life they have lived. They actively evaluate the choices they made, how they've handled the successes and disappointments along the way, and whether life seems to have had meaning and value. If they have developed a reasonable amount of the ego strengths and used them to be generative in the world around them, following values they freely chose to live by, they are likely to conclude that they had a pretty good life—that it held together pretty well. That's a sense of "integrity" about one's life.

interdependence—A comfort level with being independent in some regards, yet relying on other people to meet some of your needs.

intimacy—The experience of knowing and being known by another person. The willingness to actively reveal one's inner self to someone else is evidence of trust in the other person and trust in one's own ability to survive if that other person disappoints your hopes.

Matter Meter—A metaphorical image for a person's subjective experience of importance to another person or to people in general.

mirror neuron system (MNS)—One of two emotion systems in the limbic brain. In the MNS, neurons in the viewer's brain mimic the same neurons firing in the brain of the person actually engaged in an action or experience. This is the basis of emotional empathy—feeling what the other person feels-- and female brains typically rely heavily on this system when connecting with other people. Mirror neurons are hypothesized to be the mechanism behind "downloading" internal representations of people formative in our early lives, images that continue delivering their up-building or negative messages to us decades into the future. (See the work of Vittorio Gallese and others.)

mirroring—the idea that when a person looks into your face, they interpret your expression and the look in your eyes as indicators of your thoughts and feelings about them. How you respond to them provides them with information about themselves, their worth, and their safety. (A client report: Changing the diaper of my happy three-month old granddaughter on the changing table, I began scowling and speaking out loud my annoyance at having put the disposable diaper on backwards. Suddenly I noticed her worried look and trembling lower lip. Quickly I gave her a big smile and baby-talked her back from tears with: 'No, no, no, you didn't do anything wrong! It's silly grammy who made a mistake!) In relationships between much older children and adults, I also use the concept for actively and intentionally giving a person feedback on how you experience them.

mutuality/mutual love—Erikson's description of a relationship in which each person is devoted to the other's well-being as much as to their own. Such devotion motivates each to subordinate their tendencies toward self-centeredness.

narcissism—In the best and most neutral sense of the word, it means natural and healthy self-regard based in recognition that you matter and have value. When self-love goes awry, a person can become excessively self-centered and experience other people primarily or only in light of their relevance to them.

negative sentiment override (NSO)—Robert Weiss's term, shared by Gottman, for what happens when person A experiences person B as repeatedly acting in ways perceived as negative. When enough evidence has accumulated to tip the scales in this direction, this conclusion biases A to interpret B's actions and motives negatively even if B's behavior is neutral or even occasionally positive. The negativity absorbs anything positive. When NSO takes hold, many of A's memories of their history together may take on the negative tone and interpretation such that they actually believe there were no good times at all.

Nurture Love—Actions that communicate to another person that you treasure them. Nurture Love actions meet the other's most basic human needs in a manner that conveys that same message.

oxytocin—A naturally occurring feel-good chemical in the human brain. It is regarded as "the bonding chemical" in mammals since it plays a major role in developing trust and attachment. Tender skin-to-skin contact and mutual gazing trigger it, making it a key player in courtship bonding as well as in parents bonding with their infants. In women, a lot of it is released by nursing her baby, intimate conversations with other women, intimate unstressful conversations with males, and with orgasm. In males, tender playful contact with their baby releases oxytocin in fathers and strengthens the emotional bond. Males get a surge of pleasurable oxytocin with orgasm and it typically acts as a sedative on them in that circumstance.

pinch message (or pinch)—Sherod and Phyllis Miller's term for the often subtle yet unmistakable physiological reaction when our senses receive data we interpret in such a way that an issue suddenly exists. Life itself introduces pinches: you're late for work and see traffic backed up for an accident. Pinch. You walk into the house and smell smoke. Pinch. You taste the soup you've made and it's too salty. Pinch. The pinches relevant to love are interpersonal ones where one person says or does something unwelcome to the other person. When you don't get something you want (e.g. an expression of love on your anniversary, help with a task you're doing) or you do get something you don't want (e.g. a sarcastic remark, a demand that you do this or that) it causes a pinch, signaling an interpersonal issue has arisen for you.

Plexiglas—The idea that certain experiences cause us to 'harden our hearts' toward another person or just toward the world in general. Children are born with soft hearts, an openness to a close and trusting relationship with someone who reliably meets their needs. Trust in someone trustworthy keeps a heart soft and reachable, the equivalent of being wrapped only in thin plastic wrap. In contrast, experiencing hurts of various kinds prompts a person to wrap extra layers of protection around their heart (i.e. their vulnerable self), in order to keep hurt out and to reveal as little as possible about what's really going on inside. As this self-protection builds up, the person becomes more and more unreachable and untouchable where it really matters. At some point, it functions like a layer of Plexiglas: the person's exterior can be seen, but their interior world can't be touched.

pollinate—Bring to another person an insight into who they are as a person, information which helps them recognize something new about themselves and potentially turn it into growth of some kind.

practicing—Mahler's term for the older infant/early toddler's enthusiastic use of emerging physical and mental abilities for exploring the environment and everything in it. The young child uses the nurturer for reassurance, but is relatively unconcerned about the caregiver's involvement as they try new things.

psychological birth—Mahler's metaphor capturing her research-based observation that a secure attachment with a caregiver functions like a womb for a baby's sense of self as the brain continues to mature after birth. She saw evidence that the seed of selfhood is still gestating during the first years of a child's life within that attuned relationship and is only ready for healthy "delivery" around age three-and-a-half to four. What was only a metaphor in the 1950's has been borne out by research on the brain made possible in the 21st century by sophisticated equipment like functional Magnetic Resonance Imaging (fMRI). An attuned and available nurturer is an essential resource for a baby to learn to regulate their physical and emotional arousal.

purpose—Erikson's term for the ego strength of having a goal and being capable of pursuing it.

rapprochement—Mahler's term for the emergence around fifteen months of a toddler's increased concern about the whereabouts of their attachment figure and desire for that person to be very involved with the child. This return of a need for closeness is coupled with a continuing need for freedom to exercise freedom of movement.

rapprochement crisis—Mahler's term for a particularly important and challenging phase of a child's psychological journey of separating out of a secure attachment from an attuned caregiver. It intensifies around eighteen months and can last well into the third year as the child fluctuates between an intense desire for reunion and a fear of being engulfed by too tight a connection with the attachment figure. The caregiver's ability to remain steady and available during this time of the child's ambivalence helps the child continue to crystallize a core around which self-esteem can grow.

regrettable incidents—Gottman's term for the things that go wrong in all relationships, times we step on each other's toes or fail to empathize and take the other into account. These incidents can happen just because we're two different people experiencing a situation differently. They're more likely to happen when we are in a hurry or tired or have too many irons in the fire.

repairs—Gottman's term for efforts to restore a relationship to a good footing (Erikson would say to mutuality) after you've been responsible for a regrettable incident (see above).

resilience—The ability to bounce back from life's hard knocks.

search talk—Conversation and questions that seek information about another person's self-awareness concerning an issue. It uses open questions (who, what, where, when, how) concerning the other person's data, thoughts, feelings, wants or actions.

self (See identity)

separation-individuation—Mahler's term for the early childhood period from four/five months until thirty/thirty-six months during which a child who is (hopefully) securely attached to a nurturing person achieves a sense of being a separate person, yet still connected with that nurturing and protecting person as the reliable physical and emotional home base from which to continue developing a sense of selfhood. Ideally, the outer-world evidence of physical separateness is complimented by the timely development of internal experiences of ego strengths.

spite talk—The Millers' term for a person's communications (through words, facial expressions, tone of voice, body language, action or lack of action) that are resentful, cover hurt, and indirectly resist another person's perceived effort to control them. The spite talk style is often a counterattack intended to cause a pinch in the recipient.

softened startup—Gottman's term for a non-accusatory manner of bringing up a topic you want to discuss.

straight talk—Respectful communication that reveals information about your own self-awareness concerning an issue : the data you're reacting to, your thoughts and feelings about it, your wants regarding the situation, actions you're taken or are considering. The intent is to connect in a positive way and collaborate. (Millers)

support—Words and actions that help someone accomplish something they've set out to do.

sustain—Words and actions that help a person to survive and endure, both physically and emotionally.

teach—(See coach)

temporal parietal junction (TPJ)—one of two emotion processing systems in the human brain. Brizendine calls this the "analyze and fix it" part of the human brain, seat of cognitive empathy, and male brains tend to use it more than the mirror neuron system. The TPJ keeps a boundary between one's own and the other person's emotions, preserving more freedom for analytical thinking.

treasuring—Valuing another person so much that you experience them as a part of yourself. Treasuring inevitably begins in tender-heartedness (which may or may not be expressed outwardly in cherishing behaviors) and elevates the importance to you of the other's well-being. Over time, the experience of physical tenderness itself may come and go, but acts of devotion give evidence of continuing to experience the inclusion of that person in your heart.

trust (basic trust)—Erikson's term for a baby's confident expectation (based on experience) that the caregiver will meet their needs.

turning against—Gottman's term for an obviously negative response to another person's bid for some kind of connection.

turning away—Gottman's term for ignoring another person's bid for connection of some kind.

turning toward—Gottman's term for a positive response to another person's bid for connection of some kind. It can range from minimal acknowledgment to active engagement.

will—The inner resource of being able to exercise free choice and also self-restraint. (Erikson)

wisdom—The accumulation of knowledge and mature judgment about the issues that really matter in life. It's an ability to see human problems and challenges as part of a larger picture than just the self. (Erikson)

Notes

Introduction: Some New Glasses

1. A term coined by British psychologist D. W. Winnicott

2. See Kathy Steele, Reflections on integration, mentalization, and institutional realization. *Journal of Trauma & Dissociation,* 10[1], 1-8 cited in EM DR and Dissociation: The Progressive Approach, Anabel Gonzalez & Delores Mosquera, 2012, info@itradis.com.

3. It remains true that genuine love would foster the core ingredients valued in that different culture, so the Gottman and Sherman frameworks should still be useful in learning to love more effectively in that setting.

4. Use of *he* or *she* to avoid sex-role stereotyping or bias would be very awkward throughout a book of this type. Breaking the rules of grammar by using the gender-neutral *they* seems to be the best solution, and I will do so throughout except when certain examples require the use of "he" and "she" to designate a child and the particular parent.

5. Erikson's eight stages are taught in nearly every developmental psychology class, but as I will explain in part two, the stages and psychosocial crises of adulthood are very different from those of "the formative years."

6. Gottman's research into how relationships deteriorate shows the tipping point comes around the issue of experiencing the partner as primarily selfish. From the time that conclusion is reached, it's all downhill. *The Science of Trust*, 2011, is a scholarly tome presenting his research findings. In *The Seven Principles for Making Marriage Work and Ten Lessons to Transform Your Marriage*, he has presented the material for the general public.
7. Gottman's *Raising an Emotionally Intelligent Child* shows the link between attunement in adult relationships and emotion coaching one's children.
8. This is a reference to four mythical figures in the Judeo-Christian Bible's final Book of Revelation. Their appearance is said to signal the end of the world.
9. If a *runner* is someone who runs and a *painter* is someone who paints, it follows that a *lover* is someone who loves. Unfortunately, I can't take back the term from popular usage that has made it strictly sexual. I'm stumped for a good alternative. The love giver or one who loves are awkward, but seem the best I can come up with, for now.
10. As more is understood about the brain, many neuroscientists reserve the word *emotion* for the neurological and physiological activity prompted by an event. As those reactions take place, the conscious mind interprets them and develops a vocabulary of nuanced words for events that start out primarily as mad, bad, glad, sad or scared. In such a framework, the words for *the conscious experience* are "feelings." Like most people, I tend to use emotion and feeling interchangeably.

Chapter 1: What Do I Mean by Love?

1. Not all emotions include really clear physical experiences to help us know what we're feeling, but many do. For

instance, if I honestly report I'm afraid, my heart rate is faster than normal, my muscles are tense, and there are stress chemicals like adrenaline pouring into my system and hyping me up, preparing me to run away or defend myself. If I say "I fear Ted" or "I'm afraid of Ted," and Ted's not around right this minute, I may not be experiencing those physical reactions currently, but we both know I'm saying that when Ted is around, my brain and body are on alert, ready for action. Similarly, I can say "I love Bob" without being in the midst of experiencing in this very moment the physical sensations of tenderheartedness.

2. In his introduction to *The Four Loves*, C. S. Lewis makes this important distinction between Need-love and Gift-love (1960, Harcourt Brace Jovanavich), and Reinhold Niebuhr discusses it in an essay entitled "Man's Selfhood in its Self-Seeking and Self-giving" in *Man's Nature and His Communities*, New York, Charles Scribner's Sons, 1965.

3. Perhaps it is important to say the same thing one hundred eighty degrees differently. Devotion is when you matter to the other person in your own right—that is, your fulfillment as a person matters to them even if it means making sacrifices on your behalf.

Chapter 2: Love Builds Up, Anxiety Disrupts

1. Researchers in the field of neurology have discovered mirror neurons as the physiological component at work. Garbarini and Adenzato, 2004: Stamenov and Gallese, 2002 cited in van der Hart et al., *The Haunted Self*, W.W. Norton & Co, New York, 2006, p. 135. YouTube offers many fine explanations of mirror neurons by researchers like Dan Siegel and Vittorio Gallese.

2. It may be unsafe to imitate the behavior in the presence of the people from whom they learned it, but sooner or later, when they are with others they can get away with mistreating, it's likely to emerge.

3. Psychologist Harry Stack Sullivan regarded this imperative to avoid anxiety as the starting point of every person's self system. Even in the most loving and safe homes, children experience various kinds of anxiety day in and day out. However, if the child has little time unaffected by extreme moods of the caregivers, he believed their entire personality will form around the need to cope with those extremes. Current researchers and clinicians focusing on the outcomes of trauma and neglect in the early years have proven Sullivan right.

4. D. Wesselmann, C. Schweitzer, S. Armstrong, *Integrative Parenting: Strategies for Raising Children Affected by Attachment Trauma*, W.W. Norton and Co., New York, 2014.

5. See Richard C. Schwartz, *Introduction to Internal Family Systems Therapy*, Trailheads Publications, 2001; Shirley Jean Schmidt, *The Developmental Needs Meeting Strategy (DNMS): An Ego State Therapy for Healing Adults with Childhood Trauma and Attachment Wounds*, DNMS Institute, LLC, 2009; Sebern F. Fisher, *Neurofeedback in the Treatment of Developmental Trauma: Calming the Fear-Driven Brain*, New York: Norton, 2014).

Chapter 3: The Ambivalence at the Heart of Love

1. Several times in this chapter, I refer to *in loveness* as a temporary state of brain chemistry. I will explain that further in chapter 6.

2. Contemporary culture is in the process of discovering whether and, if so, how parents can establish themselves as the primary attachment figures in their preschool children's lives in the prevalence of extensive daycare. There is evidence that the quality of time spent together is an important factor. I think it doubtful there will ever be agreement about a minimum amount of waking high quality time needed to establish a secure attachment.

3. The commitment used to be marriage. These days, as best I can tell, if a couple living together get pregnant and decide to remain together and keep the baby, a similar mental shift may happen.

Chapter 4: The Components of a Resilient Self

1. Sullivan's work was neglected in contrast to the theories of Freud. His concepts and style are very challenging to understand and only recently have certain fields of treatment begun to mine his work for the insights it holds.

2. Brain research has established that we have two different memory systems. There is evidence that even in the womb, a baby's brain is recording experiences of sound and sensation; and as soon as they are born, visual images start being added to this implicit memory system. Around age three when we start putting words into sentences, the explicit memory system starts storing narrative stories about events that happen.

3. I have taken the liberty of modifying the racial dialect of the era. *The Help*, Kathryn Stockett, 2009.

4. In *Your Child's Self-Esteem*, Dorothy Corkille-Briggs does an excellent job of explaining the role of mirroring. New York: Random House, 1970.

5. Heinz Kohut, *The Analysis of the Self*, 1971.

6. I know many adults whose antennae are still closely tuned to a parent's signals pertaining to whether they are being a good or bad *child*.

7. See his article "Ego Distortion in Terms of True and False Self" in *Maturational Processes and the Facilitating Environment* (1960).

8. Andrew and Judith Lester, *It Takes Two: The Joy of Intimate Marriage*, Louisville, KY: Westminster John Knox Press, 1998.

9. *The Little Prince*, Antoine de Saint-Exupéry, 1943.

10. See again C. S. Lewis on "Need Love" in his introduction to *The Four Loves*, 1960 Harcourt Brace Jovanovich.

Chapter 5: Attunement—the Way to Build and Maintain Trust

1. People on the Asperger's spectrum have great difficulty with these clues. Some are oblivious to them altogether though others realize they are missing something and are frustrated they don't know what it is or how to interpret it.

2. Paul Ekman as cited in Gottman, 2011, p. 179.

3. Louann Brizendine explains current research that suggests our brains have two different, simultaneously running emotion systems: the mirror neuron system (MNS) and the temporoparietal junction (TPJ) system. The first involves feeling what the other person is feeling, while the second involves intellectually understanding what the other is feeling—without getting entangled with it—in order to solve the problematic emotion. Female brains tend to rely on the MNS and male brains on the TPJ. In *The Male Brain*, NY: Broadway Books, 2010, p 97, 166ff.

4. He monitored heart rate, respiration, sweat, and urine samples for indicators of stress levels.

5. See *Raising an Emotionally Intelligent Child: The Heart of Parenting*, John Gottman, 1997, NY: Simon and Schuster.

6. Stephen Porges's Polyvagal Theory of the nervous system is explained by Pat Ogden in *Trauma and the Body*, NY: W. W. Norton & Co, 2006, pp. 29–33. Porges's website and YouTube provide further explanations of his work.

7. *10 Lessons to Transform Your Marriage*, John M. and Julie Schwartz Gottman, New York: Three Rivers Press, 2006.

8. *The Science of Trust*, John M. Gottman, PhD., New York: W. W. Norton & Co., 2011.

9. Steven Covey's *The Seven Habits of Highly Effective Families* addresses this principle as "seek first to understand, then to be understood." FranklinCovey, St. Martin's Press, 1997.

10. I have found this and many other important communication tools in the work of Sherod and Phyllis Miller et al. *Connecting with Self and Others*, 1988, Interpersonal Communication Programs, Inc., Evergreen, CO.

Part 4: Love in Action

1. Sometimes the vicissitudes of life lead to protective walls in spite of a parent's best efforts. A child needing hospitalizations and painful surgeries, a parent's absences due to illness or injury, and various other circumstances beyond a parent's control can lead to coping strategies that make it difficult to believe in the parent's treasuring. There are therapists skilled in helping parents and children with these difficulties. See Deborah Wesselman et al, 2014, and www.ancnebraska.com.

2. In classical conditioning, two events that happen simultaneously, or very close together in time, often become linked with each other in the mind whether they were truly cause and effect or not. So, for instance, a child

who happens to come down with stomach flu the night after eating a certain meal may never want to eat that entrée again.

3. A human baby's brain at birth weighs only about 25 percent of what it will weigh in adulthood. The cells that will eventually be involved in making sense of a not-present world don't even exist until months and years down the road.

Chapter 6: Love Nurtures by Actively Cherishing a Loved One

1. For more about what fills people's love tanks, see Gary Chapman's *The Five Love Languages,* 1995, Northfield Publishing, Chicago.

2. See chapter 3 of Brizendine's *The Female Brain*, op. cit., as well as Thomas Lewis et al, *A General Theory of Love,* NY: Vintage Books, 2000.

3. Neurological action systems include those of daily living such as exploration (work, study), play, attachment, socializing, caretaking, and energy-management (sleeping, eating, homemaking) and those of defense such as fight, flight, freeze, attachment cry, and submission. *The Haunted Self: Structural Dissociation and the Treatment of Chronic Traumatization*, Onno van der Hart, Ellert Nijenhuis, Kathy Steele, NY: W. W. Norton & Co., 2006.

Chapter 7: Love Nurtures by Sustaining the Loved One

1. The fact that the comfort of human touch and interaction is necessary for survival was established as early as the thirteenth century when the Holy Roman Emperor Frederick II wanted to find out humankind's inborn language. He ordered a group of foster mothers and

nurses to feed and tend the basic physical needs of their infants but not to prattle or speak with them. In the face of drastically reduced human interaction, the infants died. Cited in *A General Theory of Love*, 2000, Vintage Books.

2. In his books, *A Fine Young Man* (NY: Putnam, 1999) and *What Could He Be Thinking?* (St. Martin's Griffin, 2004), Michael Gurian makes a distinction between empathy nurturance and aggression nurturance, observing that women tend to the first and men to the second. That's because empathic connection is central to most women's sense of self-worth, while independence and performance are more central to men's, so each is prone to give what they would value receiving. This is not true of all men and women, and many parents go against the stereotypes. And since some adults prefer being left alone when they're in pain or feel ill, if they apply the "do unto others" rule, they may make poor nurses when a spouse or even a child is incapacitated.

3. Dorothy Corkille-Briggs discusses how providing children with certain "safeties" creates their self-esteem. She uses the term *cherishing* more broadly than I use it. *Your Child's Self Esteem*, NY: Broadway Books, 1970.

Appendix B

1. Tom Holmes, *Parts Work: An Illustrated Guide to Your Inner Life,* Kalamazoo, MI: Winged Heart Press, 2007.

2. Luskin, Fred, *Forgive for Good.* New York: Harper Collins Publishers, Inc., 2002.

Works Cited and Further Resources

Behary, Wendy T. Disarming the Narcissist: Surviving and Thriving with the Self-Absorbed.

Briggs, Dorothy, *Your Child's Self-Esteem*. New York: Random House, 1970.

Brizendine, Louann, *The Female Brain*. New York: Broadway Books, 2006.

————————————, *The Male Brain*. New York: Broadway Books, 2010.

Brown, Nina W., *Children of the Self-Absorbed—A Grown-Up's Guide to Getting Over Narcissistic Parents*. Oakland, CA: New Harbinger Publications, Inc., 2008.

Chapman, Gary, *The Five Love Languages: The Secret to Love that Lasts*. Chicago: Northfield Publishing, 1992.

Conci, Marco, *Sullivan Revisited. Life and Work. The Relevance of Harry Stack Sullivan for Contemporary Psychiatry, Psychotherapy and Psychoanalysis*. Translated by Laurie Cohen and David Lee. Italy: Tangram Edizioni Scientifiche Trento, 2010, 2012, Kindle Edition.

Steven Covey, *The Seven Habits of Highly Effective Families*. New York: Golden Books, 1997.

Erikson, Erik: Erikson wrote two essays I find particularly useful for understanding his ideas about the accumulation of ego strengths. "Human Strength and the Cycle of Generations" opens with "Part 1: A Schedule of Virtues"; it appears in his

Insight and Responsibility, New York: W.W. Norton & Co, 1964.. A lengthy chapter called "Growth and Crises of the Healthy Personality" appears in *Identity and the Life Cycle,* New York: W.W. Norton & Co, 1980.

Fjelstad, Margalis. *Stop Caretaking the Borderline or Narcissist: How to End the Drama and Get on with Littlefield,* Washington, D.C.: Rowman & Littlefield, 2014.

Gonzalez, Anabel and Delores Mosquera, EMDR and Dissociation: The Progressive Approach, 2012, info@itradis.com.

Gottman, John M., PhD and Nan Silver, *The Seven Principles for Making Marriage Work.* New York: Three Rivers Press, 1999.

Gottman, John M., PhD. and Joan, *10 Lessons to Transform Your Marriage.* New York: Three Rivers Press, 2006.

Gottman, John M., PhD, Joan DeClaire and Daniel Goleman, *Raising an Emotionally Intelligent Child The Heart of Parenting.* New York: Fireside, 1997.

Gottman, John M., PhD, *The Science of Trust—Emotional Attunement for Couples.* New York: W.W. Norton & Co., 2011.

Gurian, Michael, *A Fine Young Man.* New York: Putnam, 1999.

Luskin, Fred, *Forgive for Good.* New York: Harper Collins Publishers, Inc., 2002.

---------------------*What Could He Be Thinking? How a Man's Mind Really Works.* New York: St. Martin's Press, 2004.

Holmes, Tom, *Parts Work: An Illustrated Guide to Your Inner Life.* Kalamazoo, MI: Winged Heart Press, 2007.

Kohut, Heinz, *The Analysis of the Self.* Chicago: University of Chicago Press, 1971.

Lester, Andrew and Judith. *It Takes Two: The Joy of Intimate Marriage.* Louisville, KY: Westminster John Knox Press, 1998.

Lewis, C.S., *The Four Loves.* New York: Harcourt Brace Jovanavich, 1960.

Lewis, Thomas, *et al, A General Theory of Love.* New York: Random House, 2000.

Mahler, Margaret S., Fred Pine and Anni Bergman, *The Psychological Birth of the Human Infant.* New York: Basic Books, 1975.

Miller, Sherod et al, *Connecting with Self and Others.* Littleton, CO: Interpersonal Communication Programs, Inc., 1988.

Niebuhr, Reinhold, *Man's Nature and His Communities.* New York: Charles Scribner's Sons, 1965.

Ogden, Pat, *Trauma and the Body.* New York: W.W. Norton & Co., 2006.

Porges, Stephen. Porges is a neuroscientist and most of his writings are at that complex level although some, such as "Wearing your heart on your face" in *Psychotherapy Networker* are helpful to the rest of us. Written and filmed interviews are also helpful in understanding his insights. See his website http://stephenporges.com/ for a broad array of options.

Saint-Exupery, Antoine de, *The Little Prince,* translated by Katherine Wood. New York: Harcourt, Brace and World, 1943.

Steele, Kathy, Reflections on integration, mentalization, and institutional realization. *Journal of Trauma & Dissociation,* 10(1),1-8.

Stockett, Kathryn, *The Help.* New York: G.P. Putnam, 2009.

Van der Hart, Onno et al, *The Haunted Self:* Structural Dissociation and the Treatment of Chronic Traumatization. New York: W.W. Norton & Co, 2006.

Wesselmann, D., C Schweitzer, S. Armstrong, *Integrative Parenting: Strategies for Raising Children Affected by Attachment Trauma.* New York: W.W. Norton & Co., 2014.

Winnicott, D.W. *Maturational Processes and the Facilitating Environment.* London: Karnac, 1990.